Enhanced Life Performance

Achieving the Best Version of Self

DONALD MONISTERE

outskirts
press

Foreword

The Enhanced Life Performance Program along with the Legacy Plan is a process that has been evolving over time. As much as 10 years ago, I did an annual seminar called, "How to Have Your Best Year Ever," and the sessions were always filled with people trying to improve their approach to life. People long to have a fulfilling and successful life, but they aren't always sure exactly what that means.

I never set out to write this book for the masses but as I got further along, more people asked me to publish it for those who were interested. I found out that, like many things in life, the pressure of writing a book for the masses was far too great of a challenge and I did not make much progress.

Through reflection, meditation and prayer, I found that the desire to document the process that had taken so many years to evolve was definitely there, but the thought of the time it would take seemed to far outweigh the potential for success I might experience, even if the process of publishing the book turned out to be a successful journey. The issue that I was faced with was that I had not correctly defined the real reason I should be writing the book in the first place. Therefore, I didn't have a clear and unobstructed view of the end result and who really I was writing it for.

Once I realized that I shouldn't be writing a book for the masses; instead, I should be writing a primer or set of instructions that I could give to my children so they could find fulfillment, it all seemed to fall in place. That's it! Focus on what I would want my kids to know about me and the process that I use to execute at a high level. That did the trick and suddenly the goal had become clear and well defined.

The words began to flow and the book became a passion… because my true motivation was now clear. I wanted to leave something behind for my kids—and possibly even their kids—simply to help them through life. In a nutshell, I wanted to leave a Legacy. You will read much about this in the chapters to come, and so much of it is spiritually guided with practical steps to help you create the life you want. If others are able to get something from it I am grateful, but simply put, I wrote this for my children to use as a reference guide… even after I am gone.

Therefore; I dedicate this book to those I wrote it for. Cari, Candace, Cooper and Cameron: you are my world and you made this book possible. You are all very important to me! You allow me opportunities to achieve real fulfillment. You guys are far more successful than I will ever be, and I hope that you understand that so much of who I have become comes from the hope that I can help you become who you want to be! Pops loves all of you, and I want you to know that you can have whatever you want, as long as it aligns with what the Holy Spirit has in store for you. If the early signs are any indication, He has big plans for each of you!

Table of Contents

Introduction

The concept of Enhanced Life Performance has been an ongoing passion of mine for many years, and if I remain true to the concept of the program, it will continue to improve year after year. This journey—and my slightly atypical approach to life—started when I was a very young student athlete facing the challenges that all kids tend to face as they mature. Growing up in a small city in Hammond Louisiana, I was—like so many others—picked on and bullied by many of the kids that, up until that point, I had considered my friends. Not just the normal 'ribbing' that goes on in the dugouts and locker rooms across America, this was more vicious and hateful, and it escalated to a point that became abusive, both mentally and physically. As I reached puberty, my friends became taller, stronger and faster. Even though I was talented in most everything I did athletically, my genetic makeup and ignorance of the principles of fitness, left me vertically challenged and roughly 50 pounds overweight. This occurred during my early teen years, which is not a good combination for an athlete or for a teenager just trying to get through life.

Like so many other children, I wasn't the kind of kid that was going to go home and complain about it to my parents or to the teachers, who often turned a blind eye anyway. After all, getting my ass kicked from time to time was my problem, right? Make no mistake, I was taught that life is not always easy, and at this point, standing up to bullies in school was getting me nowhere. At one point, I deduced that the reason I was picked on had to be because of my weight. In the summer of my 13th birthday, the peak of puberty, I decided to stop eating so I would no longer be the 'fat kid.' I lost 54 pounds in three months, and became very ill. Once the summer was over, I went back to school, the "fat kid," no more! Unfortunately, now I was the eighty-six-pound weakling that could barely lift his pencil, and even the athletic success I had enjoyed seemed to decline as well. I was a fairly sick child and was dealing with an eating disorder, before eating disorders were readily diagnosed. The common panacea for all things challenging teenage boys at that time seemed to be, 'Rub some dirt on it and get back in there, Monistere!' If only I had a dollar for every time my football, baseball or track coaches would send me in for the next play or the next snap completely unprepared, both mentally and physically. There was no concussion protocol or buckets of hydrating fluids. Hell, back then, they wouldn't allow us water, just to 'make us tougher.' I don't share this to place blame, mind you, that was just the way it was done back then and believe me I deserve much of the blame for not believing that I was worthy of the next snap or play. We often are 'sent back out there' in life, completely unprepared or feeling unworthy… and then wonder why things aren't going our way.

Once back in school, even after losing the weight, the bullying didn't stop. At the time, I had no idea that the weak often times become victims of the strong, and in many cases are content to allow it to happen, after all, who wants their ass kicked? This holds true for individuals as well as entire populations, but this phase of my life had run its course and I was about done being on the losing end of a bully imposing his will upon me and my life. I decided that I was going to live free from persecution, or just die fighting those who tried to impose their will on me. I wanted more!

My dad introduced me to weightlifting and martial arts, and my life began to change. I never was the kid that would back down from a fight, even one that I knew I would lose. As I got stronger and more agile, the bullying subsided and the day came when the biggest kid in school got to witness exactly what I had learned in martial arts, and just how strong I had become. The bullying stopped, but my education in fitness and the disciplines of martial arts had just begun. I became a student of the physical, the mental, and the preparation that it takes to have a different kind of Spirit, Mind and Body.

Fast forward to 1993, when I decided to start my own systems integration company, complete with multiple employees and a ton of responsibility, I knew that I had to deal—once and for all—with the feelings of not being good enough, strong enough or smart enough that lingered from the days of my adolescence. At this point in my life, I was no longer willing to only be 'good' at my career. It just wasn't enough, and honestly, the thought of being pushed around by a bigger stronger person or company that I might compete with just wasn't acceptable. So, at the age of 25, after much research and contemplation about what it took to be successful, the concept of 'Enhanced Performance' began to take shape. I wasn't looking for just a little success; I wanted a level of hyper-success that I hadn't experienced before. The intentional habit of expecting excellence from everything that I or any member of my staff attempted was necessary and my never quit attitude began to grow.

Back then, the only thing that got in the way of the excellence we displayed each and every day, was the limitation of my own expectations of how really great we could become. Let me say this one more time, because it is pretty much the root of why I had to that point allowed myself to believe that I or the people in my life were not worthy of a fulfilling life. The only thing holding me back at that time was—you guessed it—me!

So, how is that possible? Up until that point, I had been conditioned to fight through adversity and stand up to what amounted to adolescent tyranny. Many times in fact, I had won even when I lost, but the desire to remain hidden and off the radar of the strong was still a limiting factor in my life.

As I struggled with these concepts in 2008, I was approached by a larger systems integration company. They wanted to buy my company and have me come to work for them. This larger company had been a formidable competitor and just like the bullies at my school seemed to take what business they wanted back then. The concept of selling my company was a bit foreign to me, but it uncovered something within me that had been there since my days of hiding in the hallways to avoid confrontations. What value did I really have, and why would this large, successful company want me? Sadly, I realized that even as an adult with a successful business, I didn't believe that I was deserving of a fulfilled life, or the things that the strong received. The root cause of this feeling of lack of value could all be traced to my childhood, where that kind of attention and success had led to pain for me. So now, when this larger company offered to purchase my business for far more than even I thought my company was worth, I realized it was time for me to stop hiding in the hallways of Holy Ghost Catholic School, and to figure out who I really was and what I really could accomplish.

This was the secret finally revealed! Even in my attempts and in many ways success of achieving "hyper-success." I was still battling a question of value and lack of fulfillment. A total stranger saw more value and worth in me than I did, or ever had. My business by all accounts was a success but my life was not fulfilled. At that moment I decided the time had come for my world to get a little bigger... and the Enhanced Life Performance program began!

So began an all-out assault on gathering data and figuring out how I should be approaching my life, my career and my world! Enhanced Life Performance was formulated using two concepts that rarely intersect. First, I considered that a 360-degree approach to life which included mind, body and spirit was necessary in order to achieve the one thing that we are all looking for, fulfillment! Next, if we took it one-step further, one more degree if you will, to 361, we would consider the concept of continual improvement.

In other words, once we got it figured out, once we finally figured out how to balance our mind, body and spirit we could achieve fulfillment, but if we could even improve from there, we could accomplish the one thing that we all want out of life and that is to leave a lasting legacy! See, when all of the core life components are clicking along and fulfillment is achieved, we as humans have a tendency to rest. While rest is essential in order to progress further, it should only occur after we have adequately and aggressively tested the spirit, mind and body. When we rest without a sufficient testing phase, often times the balance is lost. If we fight that desire to rest at the wrong times, if we press on and continue to improve, the state of constant fulfillment becomes the norm and that state drives in us an innate desire to give back to others. We coach, we teach, we give at a level that provides even more fulfillment. When we do that, we begin to build our legacy, if—and only if—I can be fulfilled by achieving balance in the core components of my life, and not hide from those people I perceive as 'strong.'

Now, before you decide this is only about chants, meditation and connecting with the energy of the universe, please understand that— while some of that is important—the most essential thing about corralling the core components of life is determining why we are trying to achieve that in the first place. Enhanced Life Performance truly does take it one degree further than spirit, mind and body, it looks at continual improvement through the 'plan, execute, evaluate and improve' process. This program shows you how to take this well-known management concept and superimpose it on to your life. What it creates is a life worth living, worth improving and—most importantly—worth sharing with the entire world, and this is where your legend is created.

I am not just promising you a better life. I am promising you a better afterlife, and a better way of sharing the gifts—both those you have earned and those you have been allowed to have. You will have the clarity of thought, the strength of spirit and the requisite energy to accomplish this, and then share in ways that will not only impact the lives of others, but create a continuous loop of fulfillment that grows with each legacy impression. You will hear more on this concept later.

If you choose to read on, you will begin a journey you won't soon forget. The impact it will have on your life and the lives of those around you will undoubtedly surprise all concerned, especially you!

CHAPTER 1

The Why

"He who has a why to live for can bear almost any how."
—Freidrich Nietzxche

SELF-HELP BOOKS TYPICALLY bother me because they make a multitude of promises on how their particular approach or system will bring forth a massive change in life, with little consideration of how to position the person to actually make the change. Having dealt with various individuals who lack the discipline to execute even the simplest of tasks, it became clear to me that the secret to executing at a high level is not the process they use, but the person ultimately in charge of the outcome. The same message given to two similar people can manifest itself quite differently, based on how the individual chooses to utilize the message. So while I, as a thought leader, author or manager can coach or teach the process, the true outcome of the task taught is entirely up to the individual that is executing the lessons learned. I could start here and suggest that execution of a task comes down to the ability of the individual, but if we dive even deeper, we find that it isn't the *process* nor is it the *ability* of the individual carrying out the task that gets them through the really tough spots. That is not it at all. If I was doing a 'root cause analysis' of why people fail at various things they set out to do, the answer is generally very simple. All too often, they really never had an unobstructed view of why they should succeed in the first place.

At this point you may be asking yourself, "Isn't your book about the process? If so, are you telling me I don't need to read on? That all I really have to do is figure out why?" The answer is a resounding—YES! In fact, you already have everything within your mind, your body and your spirit to accomplish anything within your physical and mental capacity.

In other words, I will likely never dunk a basketball. Mainly because I am 5 foot 5, and lack the physical structure to accomplish such a feat. I do believe—if I set my mind to it—that I could possibly get to the rim, I'm just not certain I would survive the landing! I digress!

Yes, you have everything you need, but so does Lebron James, and he has a coach, and so does every other elite athlete that has accomplished great things. Similarly, and in common, they also ran a specific process of how to accomplish the task at hand, and had an accountability coach to help them get through the tedious tasks that would stand before them. Incidentally, their focus on mind and body is truly at an elite status, and they train just as we should for our own career choice. Just because we choose to sit behind a desk, or work in a trade, our training shouldn't be any less intense. Generally speaking, no one 'trains' to be good at their job once they complete whatever schooling, certification or continued education is necessary to obtain the position. What Lebron knew then and still knows today is 'The Why' of what he does. This book will not only discuss and help you find your own 'Why,' but it will also stress that we should continue to practice and train in our chosen profession, preparing for opportunities to execute at an enhanced level.

"So, if I read your book, can I be great at what I do?" Again, the answer is yes, but like all things worthy of intense study, practice, and execution, it isn't that easy.

Let's be honest for a second here, it is not as if the change from good to great has eluded you your entire life. It's not as if your whole life has been culminating around reading this book, waiting until the contents could unlock the very potential that would create majestic power over all things around you. Even I am not that egotistical, and that is a massive admonition, because my ego—once unleashed—became as big as a whale! Again... I digress.

So why is this book, this 'modus,' so different? The answer is simple, because this book and everything that makes up the Enhanced Life Performance program is controlled and governed by one thing. Not *discipline*, which you will need. Not *will* and *determination*, which is essential - and definitely not the *process* or the *tools* that I will share with you along the way. No, none of these things measure up to the one thing we must have. We have to know why! Shaping 'The Why' in your mind's eye is as important as fuel in a car, or even more fundamental... the engine or the steering wheel!

Why? When we were 4 years old, we asked this question almost as frequently as we asked for candy. We were likely told 'no' to the candy, and eventually 'no' to the question 'why!' To which we asked again... 'why?' Somewhere along the way, our parents let us know that asking why was bad. The constant 'why' questioning was irritating, and hasn't become any less so to us as adults, even though we are now looking to the heavens or asking our inner self the random 'whys' of life. Somehow knowing these answers is truly the secret of how we progress through the difficult times. Knowing the reasons why we are motivated to do what we do, makes those days when you feel it can't be any worse more rewarding to persevere through. I got my start in computer systems integration back in the nineties when computers were booming. The timing was perfect and I started my own systems integration company. Even though the timing was ideal, owning my own business proved to be extremely difficult and maddening at times.

Why? Why was I subjecting myself to the tortures of low to no cash, late nights and long hours? One day as I searched for the answer, I decided to place a picture of our children on the front page of my day-planner. Every morning I looked at that picture and it helped me define a little more clearly 'The Why' behind what I was trying to accomplish. Even then, I knew I needed a larger purpose than good cash flow or a profitable business to get through the trials and stress of making a small business successful.

This is a great example of the reality that as humans we know that our will, discipline and determination are not enough to get us through the really tough times. In addition, we need a deep understanding of why we must endure. We need to determine the source of our gratification of doing so. Too often, the thing we fail to do before we take on an endeavor is reason through 'The Why' behind it. Who has the time?

If we did truly dive deeply into our psyche on the topic of why we exist on earth today, why we must accomplish a specific endeavor, or why we should even wake up in the morning; we may find that the things we considered so important, really aren't important at all.

So what does this all lead to? It could lead to proper goal setting, which we will discuss in chapters to come. Goal setting, while extremely important, is but a mere component of 'The Why.' We must understand that 'The Why' is a concept that is more than just a set of goals that leads to tasks, which lead to action. I describe this level of understanding to be like the unobstructed focused mental clarity of a dog on a bone! 'The Why'—if it truly is 'The Why'—must shake you to your very core, and move you in such a way that if you speak of it out loud, it impacts you emotionally. This 'Why' is your life's mission statement, or what I prefer to call your Core Purpose. If I ask you in later chapters to develop your core purpose for a task or definition of your life, this "Dog on a bone" type focus is what you will need to conjure that thought. If you aren't that fixated on it, if it doesn't move you to that extent, you will not get to the place you need to be in order to find it!

Before you read on, spend 15 minutes thinking about your core purpose. We will complete a deep dive and spend time finding that core, emotionally moving purpose in this chapter, but you will find as you read this book, it becomes very clear that the reason that we do nearly EVERYTHING is because of 'The Why' and your core purpose is the outcome of knowing it.

How do I find it?

"If you can't figure out your purpose, figure out your passion. For your passion will lead you right into your purpose."
—Bishop T.D. Jakes

So how do we find our purpose? When I ask someone with kids what is most important in their lives and what they want to be remembered for, the lazy answer typically is, "I want to be a great father or mother." Even though that is noble, that really isn't our core purpose or the answer to the question. If we delve deeper into that answer and begin with the five whys of root cause analysis, it will challenge you to create a better answer. Since our families tend to be our focus and questioning that seems wrong in some way, getting deeper into that answer is necessary to understand our true purpose. The best question to ask in this instance? You guessed it—why. Why do you want to be the best dad to ever walk the planet? And, do you think that really can be measured? As I go through the five whys, you will find that while this need to be a great dad might be a component of your core purpose, it doesn't define you enough to actually be your core.

In essence, if the only sense of fulfillment you get out of life is to care for a small group of people, you are thinking too small, and you will soon be let down because you aren't the center of their universe and that is quite a bit of pressure to put on anyone. It isn't fair to your family. Please don't misunderstand me, being a great dad is noble and a necessary and serious responsibility, and should certainly be considered when developing your core purpose. It is not, however; the core of your being and only satisfies one component of the 6 areas of fulfillment, which we will discuss in later chapters. We must think bigger!

So what do I do?

"Nothing in the world is worth having or worth doing unless it means effort, pain, difficulty."
—Theodore Roosevelt

To help you with your core purpose, I would ask you to take five minutes and write down the following. Assume you are at your funeral; your family is there. Your wife or husband, your kids, your parents, your siblings and your close friends are all sitting there, and the conversation is about you. What do you want them to say about you? 'Boy, he sure could make some great bacon!' I doubt this is what you were hoping for, a lifetime of trying to be a great dad or mom, and all you get is world's best bacon cooker. By the way, you really can't screw up bacon, it tastes great even burnt... I digress.

Back to your funeral. What does the conversation sound like? Are they crying? Are they laughing? What do you want your kids to remember most about you? If it sounds a little like, 'dad/mom was always there for each of us, no matter how bad we screwed up.' Write down reliable. If the statement is, 'he/she loved us unconditionally and never asked for anything in return,' write down selfless and loving. Continue this process until you have 5 or 6 really great one or two liners that you would love to hear at your funeral. This will begin to tell you just who you desire to be. Keep in mind, this still cannot be considered our core purpose, it is merely the start of a component of your core. As we continue through this process, you will see how Enhanced Life Performance helps you to create that unobstructed, focused mental clarity—the mental picture of your core. A tangible image in your mind of what has been but a fuzzy emotion in the past now becomes a real life statement with clear and concise criteria that must be met in order to proceed toward the core purpose. How great would it be to know with such clarity, with such form and shape, exactly what we were meant to be! We each were meant to be and to do something. Oddly, the answer to the riddle of what that truly is may be already within us. No matter what your belief, be it God, a higher power or an all knowing intelligent being, it is clear to me that the answer to our core purpose was placed within us, but was intentionally made difficult to obtain because only through great trial and tribulation do we respect the fruits of our struggles.

We will continue to journey into our mind, body and spirit until we find that which fulfills us, then give it a physical representation so it can be called on at any moment of any day to motivate us through the really tough spots of our lives. This will come to our aid when simple will power and discipline fails, leaving us hanging out to dry alone at times to make very difficult decisions or sacrifices, and to act in a manner that may be counter to what our flight or fight response is asking us to do.

So let's continue our journey to discover our core purpose and the answer to 'Why!" Before we do, let's quickly review. The first thing we need to do is discover what our core purpose is.

1. *In a quiet, near meditative state, intently imagine the conversation that would be had by our immediate family at our funeral. What are the words, phrases or stories told to describe us? Summarize each story into words and write them down for later review and reflection. Remember, this is not what you think they would say today, but what you would like to hear them say if you could control it.*

Your next exercise in seeking out your core purpose will tax your memory. Try to look back on your life and remember those occasions when you were given a compliment that made you feel as if you had been lifted emotionally or spiritually… something that just made you feel great. Maybe it was a compliment about how you looked, or how you handled a situation. Jot the memory down for later review and reflection.

As an example, a work colleague once told me that many employees believed I outworked everyone in the company. He went on to talk about how organized I was. This was a time that made me feel proud of my work ethic. As a side note, I am not that organized naturally. I fought my natural tendencies because I knew if I didn't stay organized, I wouldn't be able to execute at the level necessary to achieve my goals. Sometimes we have to fight our natural inclinations in order to move past barriers. Like this process, for example. These exercises take conscious, deliberate thought and it can be difficult to continue along this path. I urge you to battle on and treat this as a journey, a mystery that you must unravel in order to find treasures beyond your dreams. Think of it like one of those Nicolas Cage movies, except at the end of this one, *you* get the treasure, *you* get the fulfillment of having accomplished something huge, and *you* get to leave the legacy! Of course Nick likely gets paid more for the movie than you will for this exercise but .... I digress!

Summarizing the next step is simple:

2. *Think back to compliments that have moved you and write them down for future review and reflection.*

The next exercise includes 5 minutes of meditation. If you have never meditated, don't get discouraged, because it really isn't that hard to do once you set aside the time to actually do it. You may find that deep meditation can help with the aforementioned exercises as well, but for this one it is essential. You may also need to do this more than once. If you are inexperienced with meditation, you may need to find a meditation guide on YouTube or do a little background study on meditation to get where we need to be. YouTube, Audible, Amazon, Google Play and others have great reference material on meditation. One of the better apps that can guide you through this process is 'Headspot.' Go to Google Play or ITunes and give it a shot.

During this meditative state you will need to conjure memories, dreams or desires that depict images of happiness. Once finished, write down the word that describes the things that were most prevalent in your mind. For instance, when I go to my 'happy place,' it always seems to be Christmas morning around the tree with my brother opening presents. In response to these thoughts, I noted the excitement of receiving gifts, sharing with family, giving gifts, embracing the spirit of Saint Nicholas, the Holy Spirit and the story of the baby Jesus. These are all things that come to mind when I think of that happy thought. This exercise is simple, but it takes intense deliberate conscious thought and very descriptive adjectives or phrases to describe the feelings are crucial. Summary:

3.   *In meditation, go to your happiest place and write down what is there. Remember, you may have to do this a few times to get a complete image.*

The people that we tend to keep company with will shape who we become. We should each have our own sphere of influence, or group of people that we call on when we need to talk through something. If you don't have a group of people you can call on, there are a number of for profit groups or associations you can use in this manner. Without a 'sphere of influence' or a close knit group to bounce ideas off of, there will be times when you feel like you are facing problems alone. I feel that having this group is crucial to further your education and establish yourself as a leader. Seek to add people to your sphere of influence who are smarter than you. For me of course, that was easy... I digress.

This next exercise takes the 'sphere of influence' a step further, and could be your first step in creating the perfect circle of colleagues to aid you in life's endeavors, but this will prove to be much more fun and creative. This is what I call my virtual sphere of influence. We are going to build a virtual dream team that you will call upon as your virtual sphere of influence to share ideas with or ask for feedback. Obviously, this feedback will come from your mind, but hopefully after considering their point of view. For instance, Mother Teresa might have a very different outlook on a situation than I would. In fact,

Mother Teresa might have a different outlook on me ...... I digress

Anyway, many people have found this to be one of their favorites of the exercises. It allows them to stretch the limits of their imagination—past the here and now—and truly decide who they get to hang out with, regardless of time and space.

Pick a person, any person, from either today or in the past that you could call upon to be your spiritual guide, your mental guide, your guide through your physical endeavors and your guide through the day-to-day tasks that you regularly undertake. Keep in mind there are no boundaries, and building a virtual team is not just creative, but it says a lot about who you are or who you want to be.

If I was going to use my virtual sphere of Influence as an example you would find David Allen as the 'task guy!' To reach out to him virtually takes knowing him a little better than you might if you only read his book, *Getting Things Done*, which I suggest reading, by the way, even if you don't take on his entire methodology. I have not myself, but his concept of not letting your inbox rule your life is incredibly liberating if you can get his system or even portions of his system to work for you. In order to put David or any other member on your virtual team, you will have to gain a deeper knowledge so you can take on his persona as you use his advice. You may try and find out if he has ever been asked the very question that is puzzling you at that time. Channeling his knowledge means you must have some idea how he might think, which will undoubtedly expand your own horizons.

I would also choose Mike Matthews, author of *Bigger, Leaner, Stronger,* along with Jack Cascio from *Twice the Speed* as my physical or athletic endeavors dream team. These guys would have answers about nutrition, supplementation, training, skills preparation, etc. Again, using these guys and mentally 'speaking for them' might take getting to know them a little better. You may even want to reach out to that individual if they are still north of the ground! You might be surprised what transpires. When I chose Mike Matthews to be on my athletic endeavors virtual team, I sent him an email. Now, I didn't tell him the part about me mentally speaking for him - after asking him questions virtually - and then answering them myself as if I were him. I was worried about him calling the cops and getting a restraining order against me or something. Damn, when I explain it like that, it makes me seem unstable.

No, this is a great idea! Really, I promise! I did tell him that I had read all of his books and loved his no "BS" way of approaching physical fitness. This actually began a dialogue via email about his research and his new supplements company—Legion Athletics. I now utilize many of his products in my Enhanced Sports Performance coaching business, and this only happened because I placed him on a make believe team. To this day, we correspond via email. Behold! My mind created a relationship that once didn't exist and never would have, had I not gone through this exercise.

So start creating your dream team and be as creative as you wish! This exercise allows you to delve deeper into their thought processes and truly attempt to determine what they would do with the situation or question you might be facing.

You may need to read some of their blogs or study up on history to find the answer, but this process will pay dividends for you that you cannot predict, because it will be specific to your team. Telling the mind that a real relationship exists actually makes it real, even if it is only in your mind. Studies show that if your mind deeply believes something, there is no difference between what you think is real and what actually is real. While this step is much more creative than the others, you will find it relatively easy to achieve. Summary:

4. *Build a virtual dream team to call upon in the various areas of your life. Who would you call upon to be your spiritual guide, your mental guide, your guide through your physical endeavors and your guide through your day-to-day tasks? Get started!*

What do loved ones think of you?

"The best times we've had on earth are usually with those we love."
— Van Harden, Life in the Purple Wedge!

This brings us to the last exercise, and it will likely be the toughest from which to get really good data. And, should you get really good data, it might be the most difficult for you to review. Regardless of what you get, I wish you luck on this because it has the potential to expose the most about who you have become to-day. If the data is accurate and you can accept it with an open mind, you will be positioned to begin a journey of change and better understanding of just how far from your core purpose you have strayed.

Here goes! Talk to those you know and love and ask them these three questions:

1. *What is my most valuable attribute or characteristic?*

2. *What is the thing that is holding me back from becoming a better version of myself?*

3. *If there was one thing you could change about me—good or bad—what would it be?*

This exercise will include you taking copious notes, but saying absolutely nothing! Do not try to explain away critiques or take any credit for compliments. This is data gathering only, and as such should be treated like any other scientific procedure. Make sure the viewpoint of the person you are talking to is untainted and un-obstructed by your opinion, because in this exercise, your opinion is not the point. Their opinion might well be skewed in some way by their feelings for you, but you need this data nonetheless, and creating a safe environment for them is extremely important.

The Results

"I pass with relief from the tossing sea of Cause and Theory to the firm ground of Result and Fact."
—Winston Churchill

By now, it is likely that there are already themes beginning to take shape, and these themes should be communicating both who you are and what is important to you. These exercises are not a magical panacea to this process or to the journey of finding out your core purpose. After all, we change regularly throughout our lifetime and today's answers could be symptomatic of a phase or troubled time that you are going through. You may need to repeat this every two or three years and search for consistency in the data. You may find another technique that is more helpful than the suggestions I have made here. Whatever the case, always endeavor to listen to what your core is telling you day-to-day, whether during a meditative state or that quiet time you may have in the car on your commute. This is the beginning of you becoming aligned with what you are really supposed to be doing with your life. We will go into much more detail on this in the chapters to come. Should you find new methods that are effective, please feel free to email me at dmonistere@enhancedlife-performance.com who knows, your suggestion might show up in my blog or on the enhancedlifeperformance.com website. I will pay you handsomely for new ideas. Wait... scratch that, I meant I am handsome and should get paid, carry on...

Once we collect all of this data, we will have enough information to better understand our purpose on earth. We should collect this data and begin to formulate what our core purpose is all about. We will start with the end in mind.

For the record, I have my epitaph already written, and the core of my being will be on display throughout this book. I want to leave a legacy, and I won't likely do it because I am the smartest guy on the planet, but I do consider myself one of the hardest working people within my circles. To provide you with an example of the process at work so that you may progress with these exercises, I present to you my epitaph. It was a product of these very exercises, but this does not mean that yours would even remotely resemble mine:

"I will stand before God knowing I have done all that I can!"

Yes, there is a story of how this statement came to be and we will cover it in other chapters, but more than anything in my life or my universe, I want to leave a legacy, even if it is only to my immediate family. I want my children's, children's, children to know who 'Pops' was, and I want to carry on the legend that is my Grandfather, since his influence still shows in me physically, mentally and emotionally. I want the legend to be bigger than life. I want it to grow with the years and for my stories to be told in the way that fables and fairy tales are told. I want them to be so highly exaggerated that they barely resemble what the truth really is. Not to feed my ego, after all, I will likely be dead at that point. I want it to be greatly exaggerated so that generations to come will listen, but in order to accomplish that, the legacy must begin now!

Can a man really run 3 successful businesses, excel in professional fighting, run triathlons and then compete in bodybuilding contests, all in one lifetime? I say yes and I hope the story grows to say that I did it better than most and did so while keeping my family first on the priority list. I want them to know that I was an accomplished author, a great teacher and coach, and did it all while riding a dragon and slaying the giant that came to earth to remove our very existence. Okay, so maybe the dragon is overkill, but the giant thing is cool!

These are all very demanding tasks and now that we have come to the end of how to find the core, I think it is worth reminding you that I wouldn't be able to strive for "Legend" status if the Enhanced Life Performance Program had never been created. I would have over-worked, over-trained, gotten sick or even died. But, because I systematically prepared my mind, body and spirit in the right way, I have and will continue to improve. ELP has allowed me to execute at this astronomically high level more consistently than I would have had I only had a to do list or a goals sheet. When those around me believe I can't possibly do more, lift more, read more, or produce at higher levels in all aspects of the three core components of life, I do! And I must admit, it is freaking sweet!

It has to be real and tangible

"This is not a plea to accept what goes against reason, but it is an invitation to discover a faith that goes beyond it. The example of Thomas is for the stubborn skeptic in us all."
—David D. Flowers

Okay, start to write down all of these recurring themes and start your journey into your core purpose by filling in these questions:

1. *In my lifetime I want to accomplish _____ _____*

2. *In my lifetime I want _____, _____, and _____ to know that I am _____.*

3. *In my lifetime I want my immediate family to know me as _____ and _____.*

4. *In my lifetime I want strangers to know me for _____.*

5. *If I could give the world one thing back (service to the community, knowledge of some topic, teaching a Sunday school class) as a thank you for all of the great things I have been blessed with and had the discipline to nurture, it would be _____.*

Once you have these questions answered, you should have the beginnings of your core purpose and that which truly moves you. We must now make this data tangible and give it life. First let's start with a clear stating of what we have found out about ourselves. Formulating your true core purpose is hard work and emotionally draining at times. You may need a break before you compile all of this data and let the concepts sink in for a week or two. I have broken down my core purpose into bite sized statements that represent all aspects of the exercises we have reviewed. I break them down to further illustrate in our mind what these core concepts mean to us and from whom they came. Then, I follow it up with a one phrase statement that I have on my T-shirts, because everyone needs a T-shirt slogan! I'd also like to have a theme song that plays when I walk into a room, but the logistics have been tough to work out… I digress.

Core Purpose (Mission Statement): Through the sweat of my brow, the God given gift of my mind and the foundations of my faith, I want to be the best father, husband, friend and man that I can be. The world has far too few real men left and I choose to do the difficult task when others choose easy. I choose to stay late when others leave early, and I choose to take responsibility when others cower. Knowing that I have done everything in my power on earth to stand before God with a clear conscience, fulfilled heart and satisfied mind will sustain my longest days and saddest moments. I will die fulfilled, having left a legacy for others to hear about and read of, and my death will be met with triumph, victory, and with curiosity of the things to come in paradise!

Epitaph: I will stand before God knowing I have done all that I can!

Family's Statement (what my family will say about me): No matter what the situation, Pops was always willing to give of his spiritual, physical, or mental strength, to make us stronger to get through what we once thought was insurmountable. God makes all things possible, Pops made us aware that nothing is impossible through God.

Stranger Statement (what strangers will say about me): By placing an extremely high value on execution, it is apparent that coaching and teaching is his gift, and he chooses to use it in a manner that makes others believe in themselves even when they believed in nothing.

T-Shirt slogan: Civilize the mind! Make Savage the Body!

This quote is from **Mao Zedong who used it in one of his speeches, he goes on to say:**

Physical education not only strengthens the body but also enhances our knowledge. There is a saying: Civilize the mind and make savage the body. This is an apt saying. In order to civilize the mind one must first make savage the body. If the body is made savage, then the civilized mind will follow. Knowledge consists in knowing the things in the world, and in discerning their laws. In this matter we must rely on our body, because direct observation depends on the ears and eyes, and reflection depends on the brain. The ears and eyes, as well as the brain, may be considered parts of the body. When the body is perfect, then knowledge is also perfect.

This speech shows us why so many people have fallen behind and accepted living an average life. The mind, the body and the spirit need to be working in unison in order to create the type of exceptional life that we all strive for. While this speech focuses on just the physical, the statement that, "if the body is perfect, so too will be your knowledge," is a flash forward into the very premise of the ELP program. In essence, we can't and we won't achieve at the highest levels if the body is not physically capable of handling the stresses that go along with it. I will expose in this book the fact that we can only leave a legacy if we have reached fulfillment and fulfillment can only be reached if the mind, the body and the spirit are working in unison.

So how do I take these items and make them physical in my mind's eye? How do I make them tangible? How do I give them substance or mass, that can be thought of, spoken of or looked at only once and instantly know what it reveals? Well, this takes us to a step that very few authors or self-help gurus will attempt, because it is hard to accomplish. Every football team has a mascot, and every movement has a hero. My life should be no different, my core purpose should be represented by something that is unrelenting, and protects the lives that it comes in contact with. For me it was easy to give it a pictorial representation. This is my core purpose and its Mascot should represent what my purpose on earth is! I am the rock that my family depends on. I am the defender of the weak, meek and humble. I must do all I can to care for them by being the most courageous—the most skilled warrior I can be. The only person that can do what I list in my Epitaph, Stranger Statement, Family Statement, and Core Purpose is the image you see here. He is a Knights Templar and it looks to me to be one of the best to ever put on the armor of God. As Christians traveled across the ever-expanding Rome, the Knights Templar kept those traveler's safe through their courageous defense of righteousness. It was said that they even guarded the chalice from which the blood of Christ was consumed. This is the image of my core. I don't always live up to the courage it must have taken to stand up to the Roman Empire, but it stirs emotion within me. This is my core. It moves me to think about what it took to be a man in this time. It moves me just to think about holding and protecting the Holy Grail, and I can be that courageous, I will be that courageous!

Now that you understand what I mean by giving your core purpose a tangible physical image that the mind's eye can fixate on when life gets tough, what is the image that you can connect to your core? So much of this book will be grounded in practicality and process related information, with tangible steps you can take to improve. Enjoy being creative with this! As you choose to make this journey, decide what makes your core tick to discover what makes you... A Legend!

CHAPTER 2

The How

"Spectacular achievements are always preceded
by unspectacular preparation."
—Roger Staubach, Quarterback Dallas Cowboys

I URGE YOU to read on, even if the mental image of your core purpose is still taking shape. Since this process tends to take time and is rather dynamic anyway, it stands to reason that through our continual improvement process 'the Why' will always be in a state of evaluation, maturation and reflection. We will jump now to 'the How' and in this chapter we will introduce concepts that have been discussed in other self-help books, but our approach will be less academic and more personal. We have spent a fair amount of time in Chapter 1 being very creative and dare I say, spiritual. While most of my writings tend to touch the soul, the next four chapters will be both practical and spiritual. We will endeavor to place functional or practical lenses over topics that have typically only been written in a spiritual manner. Much of what I have surmised is through conscious awareness of the ways life, the Holy Spirit and the universe care for us. Let me caution you that while not all of my conclusions can be tied back to scientific fact, the topics we will discuss are valid and the process we will go through works. Its existence, if you achieve a higher level of consciousness, will be undeniable. While many of the concepts that

I will introduce are a little further from the 'center of the plate' than most, I ask you to read on with an open heart and open mind, and the result will be life changing.

The 'How' that we discuss will lay the groundwork and become the base of how we execute everything we do. You have seen the physical manifestation of my core in Chapter 1. In my mind, his name is Joseph and I call on him as if he were my guardian angel. Remember that over time, Joseph has become the mental image I have created for my own core purpose, or better yet, my mental personification of what someone would look like and need to be like in order to carry out my core purpose in life. This gives me something tangible to place on something that is very intangible. The name I have given him is a memorial to the many great Josephs that have come before me. My father, both of my grandfathers, and my uncle were all named Joseph, and in many ways represent the man I wish to be. I also have a great respect for Joseph, the step father of Jesus. Without going into a detailed account of the miracle of the Immaculate Conception, and how difficult that must have been for Joseph to accept, I will tell you that his faith in both his wife and in God had to be unshakeable. As a step dad myself, I know how difficult it can be to take a back seat to someone else. Imagine the conversation, "Joseph, you are going to be a step dad because I am pregnant, and by the way, his real dad is God!" So, I guess taking him to the movies once in a while isn't going to impress him… I digress

What you will find through reading this book is our focus on 'the Why.' For nearly all men and for ninety-five percent of women, the one goal we strive for, the root cause of why we do everything we do in life, is to leave a lasting legacy that lives on past our exit from this earth. Death is unavoidable and ultimately beautiful. It is the conversion of the soul from this earthly life to a spiritual one. We all must go through it, but leaving our mark on the world before we go is the number one motivator, even if that mark is only on our immediate friends and family.

Joseph—my core—and I, can only leave a legacy with the life

we live if we work diligently to be in top spiritual, mental and physical condition. Remember that the spirit, mind and body must act in unison in order to find fulfillment in life, and we must be fulfilled in order to give back to others. We leave behind a legacy when we do for others selflessly and without desire for reward. Even though this sounds 100 percent selfless, the reward—as we all know— will show itself in many ways, but mostly as fulfillment. I find nothing more emotionally satisfying at the end of the day than unwinding with the knowledge that I have done all I could do that day to seek out balance, help others selflessly, and make real steps in carrying on the legacy that all of the 'Josephs' before me left in my care.

Before we begin down the path of shaping the spirit, the mind and the body, I want to introduce you to a concept that I call a 'Legacy Impression.' Because leaving a legacy rarely occurs during our lifetime, a legacy impression will help us to make progress toward the legacy we wish to leave.

A 'legacy impression' exists when we accomplish or experience a moment in our life when we know we have left behind an impression that will move someone emotionally, enhancing their life or their spirit in a positive way. A legacy impression will help provide fulfillment and is one building block to the legend that you will become.

Legacy impressions come in many shapes and sizes, and as we did in Chapter 1 with our core purpose, creating a physical manifestation of these impressions—instead of leaving them to float in our mind undefined—is crucial to utilizing them fully within your quest for fulfillment. If you can see the reward of becoming a legend or making a legacy out of your life here on earth, you are far more likely to persevere in that endeavor. In essence 'behavior rewarded is behavior repeated.' In order to delve further into this concept, let me give you some practical examples of a legacy impression.

A legacy impression, as stated above, is something that you have actively accomplished in your life that will leave a lasting mark on a person, place or thing. For instance, if you donated a few million bucks, and your hometown built a new library that bears your name, this is obviously a legacy impression. Most legacy impressions are not that easy to spot, and they don't have to be this grandiose in order to leave an indelible mark. Let's say you don't have that sort of coin, but still feel the need to do something and really want to support the community library. Showing up once at a library named after someone else to donate your time is NOT necessarily a legacy impression, do that for six years, however, giving selflessly teaching others during that time, and suddenly, you have left a mark on a community. In essence, it may take numerous tasks to equal one legacy impression, but when the mark has been left, you will know it and so will others. When this happens, you must record it in some physical way, so you can review it regularly. I keep a scrapbook of legacy impressions, and if it just so happened that pictures were taken, I place those pictures in the scrapbook with a paragraph explaining what the legacy impression entailed. If it was something someone emailed, print it out and keep it. If there was no physical manifestation, but you have data that suggests it happened, write a paragraph with all of the information that describes it, and if at all possible choose some visual representation of the impression and place it in your impression book.

A great example of a legacy impression happened to me recently, and it manifested itself in a simple text message that I received from my stepdaughter. Keep in mind, I rarely refer to her as my 'step daughter.' To me, she is mine. Out of respect for her father, I will mention that his donation of DNA was and is appreciated, but she takes after me. Even though some may argue that it is genetically impossible, they would quickly concede if they met her. She may not have my genetic code, but her heart and soul is a chip off the old Monistere block. So her biological dad can claim the deoxyribonucleic acid, but the spirit, soul and curious nature of my daughter came from me! I digress yet again, but in a good way. One morning I received the following text: "Thinking of you this morning and the great impact you have on everyone in your life, both personally and professionally. There are few like you, Don. We are so fortunate to call you our own! Love You!!!"

This did not come after some grand event. It was just a regular morning and she felt that she wanted to communicate what her heart was telling her. As you might imagine, this stopped me in my tracks. It was an unmistakable 'legacy impression,' and I could store that impression both mentally and physically in my legacy book. The really great thing about this selfless act that my daughter decided was important enough to carry out that day, was that it not only gave me a legacy impression, it chalked up another selfless act for her, which will nourish her own spirit and lead to her feeling fulfilled that day as she builds her own legacy.

I have a legacy wall in my book, and each legacy impression is a brick. Each brick builds the foundation. I have this image, not just in my mind, but in various places, that reminds me that I must always strive to do those things that contribute to my legacy. How you decide to portray it is up to you, as long as it speaks to you on an emotional level. I use bricks in the sturdy wall of a castle. You may use sheep, sports cars, boats or anything else, as long as you tie the image to the act of building your legacy; and, that when you see that image, you see that legacy.

So, was this legacy impression a response to a single thing that I did? Did my daughter just send this to me because I'm a great cook? No, in fact it took a long time to build up enough actions to inspire my daughter to send that to me, and I am certain there wasn't one action or event that I accomplished that allowed this legacy impression to happen. More appropriately, it was the combined actions, examples and selfless behavior she may have witnessed over time that had great power and impact on her. I have deliberately sought to make lasting memories and impressions with those around me, and not just with family. Let me be clear, I am not perfect at these selfless actions. My selfish, reward seeking ego often times gets the better of me. This entire process is about improvement and as you improve the number of legacy impressions you can chalk up will likely improve as well.

This deliberate focus on selfless behavior works for those outside of your immediate family just as well, and makes legacy possible. In fact, often times the most fulfilling gift you can receive is when you do something for a person that you don't even know. Often times their response of gratitude reaches levels that would seem contrived if you had done it for a family member and their response was the same. For example, give a stranger who is homeless $100, and you have left a lasting mark; give your son a $100 dollars and you have what he would call 'a good start.' I digress...

Leaving a lasting legacy may seem too lofty of a goal, but a legacy impression is an incremental step in that direction. Aim for a legacy impression and you will begin the process of becoming a legend. Most people reading this will see this as a tangible and visual way to know you are on the right track; plus, look on the bright side, you don't have to do the whole dying thing. I seem to continue to digress in this chapter.

Also, and you may judge me and tell me this is shallow if you like, but I like to focus on things that work for the individual that I am coaching, and in this instance, I am considering only me. I have found that remaining engaged in the process of legacy creation can be a challenge. It is far too easy to just wake up and drone on through life without making the necessary changes, or putting forth the extraordinary effort that it takes to become a legacy. I have used this in the past as a way of staying engaged, and at least for me it works! When I record 3 new legacy impressions, I treat myself to something nice. Nothing fancy; okay, sometimes it is fancy. I am somewhat of a shoe and a watch collector, so instead of just allowing myself the ability to buy the next cool watch I see, even if it is $50.00, I wait until I have amassed 3 legacy impressions. Yes, I did just lose like twenty man-points by admitting that I collect watches and shoes, but if cash flow is good, and I collect three legacy impressions, I treat myself. Shallow or not, it motivates me to do more, and that is how a legacy begins to build!

Regardless, of how you treat yourself, legacy impressions are a major part of the Enhanced Life Program. I review them monthly with my clients, and the secret is, you must start doing this now and your attempts must be deliberate. Until you get accustomed to doing this regularly, you may need to schedule a weekly near-term goal, such as a 'do something special for a stranger,' or 'find a way to help a friend.' This will keep the concept in front of you, and when the time arises, you capitalize on it. Is it wrong to schedule spontaneity? I choose to believe that it is not. Rarely, if ever, do we take advantage of those moments where selfless acts live if we are not predisposed and ready to do so. Don't get caught up with the idea that it always has to be a selfless act, either. Many legacy impressions are not always selfless and are sometimes driven by ego, (think back to library named for the benefactor). Donating to the library was likely done with the intent of having it named after that wealthy individual. Keep in mind though, that the 17 year old high school graduate that is using that library to prepare for his ACT, or is continuing their education utilizing the free books that they can check out, actually sees it as 100% selfless on the part of the person making the donation. Those people do not care that you got an ego boost the day of the ribbon cutting. You could be a real clown of a person, but they only care that you gave them an opportunity to improve.

So, making others better at something is lasting, and you will be remembered for it. This discussion always takes me back to when Allen Iverson had his diatribe on practice. One of the statements he made was, "How am I gonna make my team better by me practicing... we talkn' bout practice." Classic! If you have never seen this, fire up You Tube and give it a watch. Trust me, it is there, and it is worth the 5 minutes. Digressing yet again!

So, how is doing something for a stranger going to help you become a legend? This is one of those infallible truths that just seem to be on our side, regardless of the lack of science to back it up. What I will propose as science is the fact that an object in motion tends to stay in motion, and selfless acts seem to capitalize on one another. It can be explained in the various texts that exist about the laws of attraction. Books like *As a Man Thinketh* and *The Secret* all speak to the positive energy that is created when you remain in a purely positive frame of thought and seek out opportunity for selfless acts. It is my assertion that if you begin to selflessly give of your time to help others, if you couple that with a clear and unobstructed view of what you wish to accomplish in your life, then God, the universe, angels whatever you prefer to believe in just seems to provide you with exactly what you need to continue your selfless behavior.

Evil lurks on every corner

If you were paying close attention, you noticed that I suggested that God and the universe will be in alignment with your goals once it is clear that your intent to be selfless is genuine. In essence, when the acts become real and truly selfless, the alignment happens quickly.

Keep in mind, because I am an 'out of practice' Catholic and Sister Mary Helen would not allow me to believe any other way in middle school, I do believe in good and evil. While you do receive that with which you ask for during these times of selflessness, evil does have a way of creeping in to tell you that you can't and are not making a real difference. The success that you might be feeling is in fact sinful. See, I do not believe that success itself is evil, especially those who meet my definition of success. Evil finds successful people and tries to either take credit for the success, or get you to stop doing whatever made you successful in the first place! Evil will try and convince you that putting forth selfless attempts to help others to improve their spiritual lives, mental lives or general well-being, in some way will ruin your own.

If you have engaged in selfless acts, you have no doubt witnessed this evil in the form of people trying to put down your efforts. "If you do that for them once, they will always expect it," is an example of the kind of things you will hear during these times. These people—while they may not be evil themselves—are used by evil to try and change you. Evil has a way of ruining the most well-intentioned plans, and the gift of free will allows us to hear evil out and make a choice to listen or not.

Incidentally, people who are working the Enhanced Life Program and have a clear unobstructed view of what they must accomplish to be fulfilled and leave a legacy, find free will a gift! Those who do not have that unobstructed view might see it as a constant temptation that is often times insurmountable. Remember, it is only my opinion—which has been formed through countless meditation and prayer sessions over the years—but both good and evil does exist, and in many ways must exist in order for the universe to stay in balance. Human nature is to resist perfection. The plight of the artist is often not when to start his masterpiece, it is when to stop! We always try to improve on perfection, and in many ways this is our fatal flaw. A world that is perfect is a condition, not of this time and place. So don't try to make the world perfect by ridding it of evil, just make the world better by telling evil that it has no place with YOU! I do believe perfection will have its reign! I believe Sister Mary Helen called that heaven, but for today, evil must exist and we must be prepared to recognize and resist it.

Enjoying Reward is not sinful!

Those who are great at delayed gratification often struggle dealing with the enjoyment of rewards. Discipline to put off the reward will often times make it feel awkward when it is finally time to enjoy the reward you have delayed. For those who have this issue, you should consider that the reward for utilizing the very gifts that were given you is not sinful or glutinous. On the contrary—in my view—the sin is not using the gifts that have been given to you. Ward off evil and don't let your core succumb to those who say things such as, "Don't go workout today, don't eat right today, give yourself a break. Why are you volunteering your time?" Positive influences in your life prepare you and move you down the road toward fulfillment. Evil wants you in chaos and turmoil because then you are focused on only you, and you have no sense of community and reflection. You are just trying to get through the day. An approach of 'I have to get through the day' is very single minded and selfish. This is what people who are going through traumatic experiences might need as their focus, but it should not be the type of attitude that we have to get through day-to-day life. The result of 'get me through the day' may end in a completed day, but will never end in a completed and fulfilling life. Seek out community! Seek out love and reflection! If you do, there is no room for the sin of gluttony or pride to creep in, because your own excess becomes someone else's gain.

Mind, Body & Spirit

"Mind, Body, Spirit is in the wrong order; it starts with the Spirit, and nothing is worth winning if you lose or never had your Spirit"
—Donald C. Monistere

In later chapters, we will take each of life's core components that lead to fulfillment and dissect them to maximize our ability to impact each of them positively. Breaking them down to their most basic components will allow a more focused approach for improving each. We will introduce each one and then list the steps of how we approach continual improvement for each.

Now that we have a good understanding of how a legacy is built and what it means to garner a legacy impression, let's move on to a practical approach to the discussion of Spirit, Mind and Body.

The Spirit

"Great spirits have always encountered violent opposition from mediocre minds."
— Albert Einstein

From what I understand, Mr. Einstein was a pretty smart guy, and his quote above supports the concepts that I have put forth about evil.

I don't agree, however, that it is the mediocre mind that opposes those with great spirit; instead, I believe it is an overall weakness of the three core components that make us susceptible to the desires of evil. Of course, evil opposes those who choose to improve, especially improvement of the spirit.

For many, the mind and the body are more tangible and easier to grasp than that of the spirit. The subject of Spirit conjures many thoughts for different people, and while I connect my Spirit directly with my heavenly Father and Jesus, a more simplistic way for others to consider the Spirit is just the concept of 'well-being.' It is my assertion that the general feeling of well-being is controlled by your own spirit and soul. I have been quoted as saying that 'the soul should be protected as if it were a child' and the intent of the statement is to illustrate that the soul is susceptible to various inputs that our core purpose should help us to avoid. For me, Joseph is the protector and keeper of my soul and spirit, and at all cost he will protect it from negative input and evil influence. We have total control of what we allow in. First, be careful of what you allow to reach the soul, and second, feed the soul only with the nutrition of positive input. Without question, once you begin improvement of the spiritual aspects of your life, there will be far more people trying to bring you down, than those who are supportive of your improvements.

Again, my assertion is not that evil lurks on every corner, trying to thwart the efforts of the good. What I am saying is that through criticism and pressure from those around you, evil will try to make it easier to return to a less disciplined approach than working to care for the soul and your spirit. One final note, if it seems that as you improve your approach to the spirit, things begin to happen that may seem negative at first; I would argue that you are headed in the right direction. Once this negative energy sees that you are determined to not allow it to change your approach, it will move on and let you reap the rewards of your focused approach to the spiritual world, and all that it has to offer. This negative energy has a way of finding those that are trying to improve, and throwing curve balls at them until it can get them to stop. Don't stop! Once you prove that this is no passing fad and it is a new habit forming, this negative energy will soon move on and look for someone who is a little less dogged in their approach.

Give me the Step-by-Step Guide Already!!!!

So what are the practical steps to finding the hidden powers of the Spirit? We will introduce 3 steps in this chapter with details in the chapter to follow. These steps seem simple on their face, but just as you found the exercises to find your core challenging at times, this will likely be no different.

Find the Center — First, we must find our center, the ancient arts might call it your 'Qi or Chi.' As you may know I have studied various forms of martial arts, this 'Qi' is one of the most sought after realms of the Asian culture. Qi is—as mentioned above—about the soul. Qi will be described by the various religious and martial artist teachers as well-being.

As it turns out, the center of our physical body truly is in the area of the heart, and it is not an accident that when we think of the physical placement of the soul, we think about our chest or torso area. This truly is our physical center, but what we are looking for— and will develop through various exercises—is the center of our supernatural being or the soul. Through this centering of the soul and body, you will undoubtedly call upon the spiritual as a result. We will have more on how to do this in the next chapter.

Enhance its Control — In order to gain all that is necessary and good about the Spirit, we must allow it dominion over the physical. Our nature is to only allow our mind this control or dominion over ourselves, because we believe that our discipline and control comes only from our logical mind. If it wasn't for the body, discipline would be easy. The fatal flaw here is that the logical mind will often ratio-nalize or justify things that are not in our best interest to satisfy the

31

wailing and crying of the body. If this were not true, no one would ever eat potato chips…… I digress! The Spirit, on the other hand will not, and in fact, cannot accomplish this. The Spirit works in unison with the rest of the universe and places us in the perfect position to accept it's (His) grace. Our bodies and minds are the ones that jack that up (scientifically speaking.) Allowing the Spirit control and dominion over our lives, is like handing the race car over to an Earnhardt, saying, "Drive dude, just drive!" (For the record, I can't reside this close to Talladega without using an Earnhardt reference, it's like a law down here…. Free Bird!… Digressing…)

Improve the Connection – the Spirit is humble. While my core purpose is to leave a legacy, and Joseph is the strong protector of that purpose, I see my Spirit more like an image of a young Jesus who has the knowledge of God, the curiosity of a child, and the wisdom of a cleric. In order to get access to this perfect trifecta, I must strengthen my connection to it. Just like re-creating the neuropathic access to muscles after surgery or an accident that has forced us to execute some array of rehabilitation, we must work those pathways in order to gain access to the Spirit.

In the next chapter, we will break down each of these bullets that allow us to have a deeper connection with the 'Spirit' component of our core. Just as a reminder, the physical manifestation of Joseph, the image that I choose to think about when I am dealing with questions of my core, is this strong protective warrior. Questions about who I am or how I am supposed to react all start with that image. Keep in mind, the armor is the outermost layer of my core, and the inner layer is much more docile, loving and caring. Joseph has a deep intimate relationship with my spirit. Joseph is the protector of my soul and the intentions of legacy, but he knows that his very existence is governed and controlled by the very soul he protects. A true symbiotic relationship and he knows it must exist. The soul in my mind's eye is a child that must be protected, and Joseph does an amazing job of ensuring the safety of the soul because he knows that he cannot survive without the energy that manifests itself through the nourishment that the soul receives from the Holy Spirit. I will break this down more clearly in chapters to come but you will need to understand this part of how the Holy Spirit works to impact your own spiritual characteristics.

This may be a little hard to follow, but this process of defining the spirit and the physical imagery is important because things will get tough in our lives and we need to clearly understand what our spiritual nature is all about. It is easier for me to utilize Joseph the warrior to fight off issues of lack of discipline instead of little old me. I'm 5 foot 5 for Pete's sake... I digress.

This imagery may still seem a bit out of place to you if you have never done it, but the more physical, tangible and real we can make these concepts, the easier it becomes to call upon them and accept their truths.

One last note, finding one's center is a difficult task to accomplish, especially to those who have never done it. The center of our bodies resides in the torso or the area of your heart, and if we describe something that comes from the core of ourselves, we say, "It came from the heart." The heart is the most important organ the body has, but it must work in unison with all the other systems in the body in order to prosper. It is no accident that we think of the soul and its spiritual output as 'the heart' of the spirit, mind, body connection, and while it has to work in unison with the Mind and the Body, without the soul becoming healthy through a conscious attempt to have communion with the Holy Spirit, we cannot sustain life. The heart is the physical center of our body and the soul is the spiritual center.

Even those that do not believe in a higher power, in some way recognize that the Holy Spirit guides them. They just can't quite reconcile that the Holy Spirit is doing it and plays such an integral role in their lives. Sometimes we must realize and accept that not having proof that something works is not proof that it doesn't.

The Mind

People often mistakenly place too much focus on the brain as the provisionary of mindfulness. I would suggest that you look at the brain as the power source and processor only, because mindfulness and the soul (which we will discuss in detail in the next chapter) is of the entire body, not just the brain. Our being goes through three stages of mindfulness that we will discuss in detail in chapter 4.

These stages include:

Awareness – Knowing *something* is there.

Consciousness – Contemplating how you might engage or interact with that *something*.

Integration – Engaging that *something* and becoming integrated with it.

Our mindfulness must travel through these states to be truly present and truly exceptional.

And lastly....

The Body

The Body is the vessel that carries mindfulness and our spirituality from one place to another. The trials that we will go through to achieve this exceptional life will be difficult and challenging to the body, and placing it in the proper condition to be accepting of this life is not as easy as one might think. There are three components of the body that we must consider in reaching these levels of excellence and is for many the most difficult step.

Exercise and physical exertion – We must, at every stage of our life, act as if we are training for battle. In essence we are, because we will be bombarded with negativity that will try to bring us to accept mediocrity as normal. We will need to be strong to fight this urge. The body seeks comfort, and it is free will that allows us to choose it.

Nutrition – Food is medicine! What we eat may be the biggest contributor to mediocrity in today's western world. Oftentimes I see the things that we eat as methods of control that others have placed in our lives to keep us from rising above the rung on the ladder that they have chosen for us. Don't fall for it. Nourish your body as the soul nourishes the mind. You don't "need" convenience foods or foods that do not nourish your precision instrument called the body.

Rest – Sleep, and more importantly, rest, is essential to repair the daily damage that we do to our physical existence. The soul is metaphysical and supernatural, and doesn't require rest, but the body is of this earth and will turn to dust. It needs to rest, and it needs time in between battles with negativity in order to recharge and truly be present in an exceptional life.

CHAPTER 3

The Spirit

"You have to be able to center yourself,
to let all of your emotions go.
Don't ever forget that you play
with your soul as well as your body."
— Kareem Abdul-Jabbar

I WAS A Boston fan and didn't have much love for Kareem. I always wondered why that dude was so powerful on the court with little or no weight behind his enormously tall frame, and then I saw him fight Bruce Lee in *Enter the Dragon*. At that moment, I became a Kareem fan and even though I still pulled for Boston, I wanted Kareem to do well. That being said, Kareem had practiced martial arts and spent quite a bit of time mastering 'Qi' aka 'Chi.'

Finding the Center

For the purposes of this book we will spell it 'Qi.' Loosely translated, Qi means life force. As defined by Vocabulary.com, Qi means: "The circulating life energy that in Chinese philosophy is thought to be inherent in all things. In traditional Chinese medicine, the balance of negative and positive forms in the body is believed to be essential for good health."

I had a great opportunity to compare and contrast how the Qi can be used to help align all things around you and focus yourself on one goal or endeavor. As a martial arts instructor, we meditated and focused our energy almost daily. If you were to study Tai Chi you would know that Tai Chi involves using the energy of the universe to harness power and wellbeing. Tai Chi suggests that the universe is made up of positive and negative charges (yin/yang) with the positive coming from the ground and the negative coming from the air. You must use both in conjunction with one another to achieve wellbeing and become centered. This is no different than our discussions so far about fulfillment through proper engagement of the spirit, the mind, and the body. Qi focuses in on the spiritual part of the three core components. Ancient texts that speak of Qi seem to support the notion of good and evil. In essence, in order to harness the energy of the Qi you have to harness the energy of the positive and the negative, not just positive alone. As a Christian there is only so far I can go with the use of Qi because I gain my stability or balance in my life through the Holy Spirit, but I am presenting a secondary source and system of knowledge that also suggests that good and evil exists.

Good. Evil. Yin. Yang. Qi. All of these concepts cite the existence of both positivity and negativity existing in our universe and how it interacts with us as patrons along for the ride. I have experienced and witnessed the best of the good and the worst of the evil, and evil is nothing to play around with. While I have never been consumed or possessed by evil, people close to me have and it is very real! Maybe not in the way depicted by Hollywood, but the evil that prowls about the world, in my opinion, looks around for and exploits those who are 'off center.' Evil does exist and manifests itself in much subtler ways than you might expect. Kevin Spacey played a character, Roger Kint, in the 1995 film, *The Usual Suspects*, delivering one of my favorite lines speaking to the way evil really works. "The greatest trick the devil ever pulled was to convince the world he didn't exist." This is how evil attacks us... in ways that we can't or don't want to see. At least, this is how it has been for me. Others will cite a much more aggressive display by evil, which I have witnessed among family members in the not so distant past. Things that we write off as simply a 'lack of discipline,' can be attributed to a negative energy source bombarding you with improper messaging, until you become weak and lose focus on your goal of achieving the optimal self. In this instance, the outer self finally gives in and evil gets to blame the entire matter on you. Oddly enough, evil must exist in order for the universe to prosper. Some people struggle with this notion, but Qi may be an easier way of looking at it. Instead of good and evil, it may be more palatable to concede that in order to find our center; we must be grounded in positively and negatively charged environments. The science behind this is fascinating, but I dare say the scripture behind it is even more engaging.

Take the time to read the following verses, Matthew 12:33-37; *"Either make the tree good and its fruit good, or make the tree bad and its fruit bad, for the tree is known by its fruit. You brood of vipers! How can you speak good, when you are evil? For out of the abundance of the heart the mouth speaks. The good person out of his good treasure brings forth good, and the evil person out of his evil treasure brings forth evil. I tell you, on the day of judgment people will give account for every careless word they speak, for by your words you will be justified, and by your words you will be condemned."*

There is recognition that evil resides in us. "How can you speak good when you are evil," suggests that there are times when we may be evil and times when we are not. The key part of the phrase is 'when you are evil' in essence validating that we can vacillate between both states. If we allow, evil will come from our being, if we remain focused on the Holy Spirit and the humility He brings, we will 'bring forth good.'

Overlay that on top of the study of Qi and the science behind harnessing energy and you will have the begininings of an understanding that suggests that in order to gain control over our universe, which has both negative and positive energy, we must become skilled at controlling both! Before you assume that this is where the book derails into a strange place of mythology, I would argue that almost all established religions speak of good and evil existing on the same plane, and our ability to harness the one while being mindful of the other is one of the key concepts that allowed me to find this 'Enhanced Life' that I have spoken of.

The hard part, as we mentioned in the previous chapter, is not tapping into the Spirit, it is allowing it dominion over the other core components and letting what seems like an illogical entity act in what we often think of as a logical world. There is no magical power granted to those that understand that all may not be exactly as we see it. I do believe, however, that your reality can be drastically improved if you know a few simple truths.

These truths are:

1. The Holy Spirit or the Universe wants to help you, but only if you engage it positively!

2. The Spirit has dominion over the universe!

3. The Spirit does not make mistakes, you do!

While the laws of gravity and other irrefutable concepts are part of our world, the idea that the fate of our lives has already been lived and we have no impact on this life is, in my opinion, false!

"You create your own universe as you go along."
—Winston Churchill

As Mr. Churchill properly conveys, each of us have control over the positive and negative energy in the universe, and if we recognize how to utilize both the good and the bad, we can live a happier and a more fulfilling life which will ultimately lead to a lasting legacy.

For those of you who have studied the laws of attraction, if you can focus your attention on the positive energy that exists in the universe, you will attract more positivity, but the negative, while further from your core, never goes away. The practice of manipulating both your positive and your negative life force is what Tai Chi is generally about, and to achieve center you must embrace the positive, acknowledge the negative, though not letting it infiltrate the space that is your center. So, what is the negative's job and how do we use it? The key to using it is just acknowledging that it is there and recognizing when it is trying to infiltrate the positive space that you have created around you. It is there because of some basic principles of free will. Again, regardless your faith, we all must agree that we have been granted the right to choose between good and evil. Evil or negativity has its own power, but it is kept in check by the orchestrator of the universe. We are not meant to understand why, but I choose to believe the reason for free will is similar to the way I would want my friends to choose me. I want my friends and family to love and respect me because they choose to, not because I forced them to. For me, that will suffice my curiosity on the topic of why evil must be here. Yes, there are deeper biblical accounts that explain this phenomenon, but I don't need any more clarity than that of God's desire to be worshiped by choice, not by force.

Using negative energy for positive gain is a simple concept, but can be difficult to first recognize and then do something about. I call it 'the push method.' We attract energy that vibrates at the same frequency as we do. If we are displaying negative feelings and emotions, we attract negative feelings and emotions. You have walked into a room of people where something bad has happened and you can sense it. This is how negativity infiltrates all in its presence and conversely how 'push' works. The way to use the negative against itself is to reverse the process. Simply stay in a positive energy state and the negative will 'push' away from the area of your being and its surroundings. Have you ever been impacted by a really positive up beat guy or gal? Have you ever walked up to people who were laughing so hard that you started laughing too, even though you had no idea why they were laughing in the first place? This is the opposite effect of the aforementioned example, and it is just as powerful. That is 'push' and whatever you are attracting—positive or negative—not only can impact you, but it can impact others in your vicinity. If you vibrate at a frequency that only positive energy is attracted to, the universe and your body must make room for this energy by ridding itself of the other forms of energy sources. The positive energy engulfs you and the negative is pushed away.

The further the negative energy is from you, the sooner it becomes nothing more than a spectator of what you have become, which is a being surrounded by pure, clean positive energy. The stronger and more developed that energy source, the harder it is for the negative energy to penetrate its outer layer. Imagine yourself inside a protective field where evil and negativity cannot reside. In essence, if your glass is half full with positive energy, you are leaving an available space for other forms of energy to fill it up, and if you are not careful, it could become the predominant energy source. Now negativity is driving the life bus, typically off the first available cliff, metaphorically speaking of course...I digress.

For the record, this concept came to me after much research on the laws of attraction. As I surrounded myself with positive energy during my meditation session, I got the distinct feeling that the negative area around me was being pushed away, and with each positive thought the feeling became even more empowering. This feeling can be corroborated in the famous texts that we know like, *Think and Grow Rich, The Secret, As A Man Thinketh,* and many others that try and explain how the laws of attraction work. This seemed a bit simpler for my southern mind to wrap around. In short, think and be positive and the little room you had reserved for negativity becomes full, in effect forcing it to leave.

This thought or concept has opened many doors for me. Since I stopped trying to beat or fight the negative energy, I just became more focused on the positive and continued to focus on the centering of my being, which to me is a mindful attempt at emptying the mind and body of all feelings, and then, replacing it one by one with exactly what I want at that moment.

Remaining positive among the negative impulses that surround me, I recognize that the negative influence moves further away. The negative energy is not gone, mind you. In fact it is there and present to witness that I ignored the negative and did the right thing. My mental imagery places evil as the spectator of the good, and it must sit and watch as it realizes that its efforts were beaten due to an acceptance of the good and positive, not an assault directed at the negative. I also believe that for every successful thwarting of the negative, the less it will try and infiltrate your positive space. Again, evil moves away from you, it doesn't leave. Evil will move away, hoping that you forget it was ever there, waiting for that day that you are weak and falling back into the habit of allowing the negative in through one of the seven deadly sins. The seven deadly sins are all gateways to the evil that surrounds us. Lust, Gluttony, Greed, Laziness, Wrath, Envy and Pride are all listed in biblical text as the 'detestable' sins. These sins are detestable because they invite evil and negativity to lay waste to your positive self, and ultimately are difficult to recover from.

Instead of concentrating on the 7 deadly sins, we should endeavor to focus on the 6 areas of life fulfillment, which are Faith, Family, Career, Finance, Community and Charity. I find ways to bring positivity to these 6 areas of fulfillment instead of fighting away the negativity of the deadly sins. This is how evil is beaten. There will be a time—that has already been written about—where we will fight evil directly, and while we should not focus on this today, trust me, I plan to be on the battlefield!

Evil is not the way Hollywood and others want you to believe it to be. The church has made a mint depicting it as fire and brimstone, making you frightened of it. Make no mistake, evil is real and scary when it is allowed to run the body, but the majority of the public will never experience evil this way at all. They will experience it as that little voice that says, "Go ahead, one doughnut won't hurt!" If we enhance the control of the Spirit to nourish the soul and have control over the mind and the body, utilizing the universe's power becomes far easier.

So what does this have to do with finding the center? The answer is absolutely everything. In order to find your center, you must understand what must reside within, and more importantly, remain on the outside of that center. Positive emotion feeds your ability to center your being and negative emotion tends to make this extremely difficult. Finding the center is as much about understanding what the center is, as it is the act of finding it.

The Holy Spirit to me is the Master of the Universe—God—who is in the spiritual or supernatural realm. It is the Holy Spirit that I call upon in meditation to nourish my soul, which is the supernatural immortal part of me that creates my spiritual attitude and characteristics. This is what I know of as 'my spirit.' (Explanation: "my spirit" is different than the Holy Spirit; The Holy Spirit is God, "my spirit" is the product of my soul and the outcome of me seeking community with God.) This explanation shows that there are three distinctly different components of spirituality. The Holy Spirit, which is God (or the Universe to non-believers), your soul, which I will argue in this chapter is truly the metaphysical part of our body that creates (with The Holy Spirit and your help) your own spiritual characteristics that then becomes your spiritual landscape! The illustration below shows the Holy Spirit impacting the soul that creates the output of our own spirit.

The soul is that center we have been speaking of, and as I mentioned above, we should seek during prayer and meditation to empty our soul of all energy and emotions, thereby getting rid of any evil and replacing it with all of the positive things we wish to focus on. This is the act of centering one's being and bringing it in line with what God wishes for us. There will be more on this topic later in this chapter. Now that we know where and what the center is, we must find what we are really trying to accomplish with it. You are engaging the Holy Spirit to nourish your soul into a strong supernatural force that can't be messed with by negativity or evil! Asking the Holy Spirit, who controls the universe, to help you nourish your soul to thwart evil that resides in the universe, sounds like we are playing with a stacked deck, and in actuality, we are. The simple fact is that far too many people never ask for this nourishment, nor do they put themselves in a position to receive it.

Your physical center, as depicted in the illustration, is truly the area of the heart, and the supernatural soul resonates from the center and, I believe, engulfs your entire body. In meditation, utilize the imagery of the center of your body as your soul, and the bright white light emanating from that region is creating a protective veil over your entire body. Once you can visualize this, you will find your center and be able to move to the next step.

Enhance its Control

In order to gain all that is necessary and good about the Spirit, we must allow it dominion over the physical. Our nature is to only allow our mind this control or dominion over ourselves. The fatal flaw here is that the logical mind will often rationalize or justify things that are not in our best interest. The Spirit cannot accomplish this. The Spirit works in unison with you and the rest of the universe, placing us in the perfect position to accept its grace. The grace of the universe is on display every single day. My faith tells me that this grace is granted by God, but you do not have to be of my faith to witness the grace of the universe. Trees grow toward the sun;

Camels carry adipose tissue only in their humps, because if they carried it throughout their body the insulation would kill them in the heat. Some call it evolution; I call it the revolution of universal grace, brought about by God himself.

Our minds are the enemy when it comes to the grace of the universe, and our bodies are not prepared to fight this battle alone. Allowing the Spirit control and dominion over our lives is like handing the race car back over to an Earnhardt and saying, "Drive dude, just drive!"

So how do we hand the race car back over to the Earnhardt's? As you might imagine, meditation or prayer is a key component of how to accept the power of the Spirit, but regardless of your faith, one of the best Spirit instructors is Jesus Christ. Okay, before I lose all the non-Christians, let me just get this out in the open. I believe we can all agree that Jesus is either who he said he was, or he is one of the baddest dudes to have ever walked the earth. Okay, I guess there is room for just being bat spit crazy (my mom wants me to take this part out) but bat spit crazy will rarely change a world positively, because it takes discipline. My belief would be that those who are crazy can't and don't have the mental faculties to achieve Qi, or balance to a level that would allow them to accomplish what Jesus did. So, if we used his example, we can add a few things to the list that will allow us to be more closely aligned with the Spirit. We must have a high degree of confidence and be well educated as Jesus was. Remember, he taught in the temple at age 12, but more importantly than knowledge, we must be selfless and humble. Humility is the key! Jesus cornered the market on humility and there is no one who has commanded the strength of the Holy Spirit as much as he did. No way does he endure what he did without it.

I don't know why the Spirit loves to reside with people who are humble, and I am not sure if this fact is causal or correlated. Is being with the Spirit and allowing Him to drive the mind and the body causing us to be humbler, or does the spirit migrate to those who already have this trait. Regardless of the reason, if you seek to be selfless and humble, the Spirit will find you and accept dominion over your mind and body, and this is exactly what we want.

With humility and selflessness, seeking out how you can help others is a great step in finding your spiritual center, and the connection to 'The' Spirit. So in a practical manner, how do we accomplish this centering of Qi or 'our' spirit? I will list three steps that can be helpful, and while they are easy to write, they are difficult to accomplish consistently. Let's visit the three steps that you need to take to let the Spirit enhance its control.

Meditation – We have touched on meditation briefly, but this is a very important part of how we allow the Spirit dominion over our mind and body. In Chapter 2, we went over how to prepare for meditation, and taking a class is actually a really good idea. Yes, you may meet some really strange people in 'meditation class,' but keep in mind that it is a two way street, and that the really strange cat lady in the class may go home and tell her cats that you are a complete piece of work and will never find your purpose… I digress.

Meditation, more than anything takes time. I have learned that there are certain things that help me enter into a meditative state, allowing me to create the best possible outcome. One of those things is cleanliness. Now, my mother always said that cleanliness was next to Godliness and that there is no excuse to not smell good, because water is free and soap is cheap. (This was back when water was actually free.) When I get out of the shower, I seem much more connected with the power of the Spirit. Keep in mind some people prefer just the opposite, but for me this works. Loose fitting clothes and a cool place to rest are those environmental properties that aid me in entering the meditative state that works best for me. Keep in mind; this truly is prayer for me. I typically pray every night, but that prayer is more of a conversation with God, asking for the many things that we as humans feel are important. Protection for my family, health, and the other things that we see as important in life are typically the topics of that conversation.

My meditative prayer is more intense, and allows me to enter into a feeling of community with the Spirit and the universe that he has dominion over. This state allows me to not just be a part of that universe, but to be in that universe where the power of every living thing can be harnessed to achieve a centering of my own spiritual awareness. When I achieve this state, and it doesn't always happen, I feel safe to let the Spirit 'take the wheel' and nourish my soul. Through this I can impact the mind, and the body in the direction that is in the best interest of my life. Incidentally, purity of mind and body helps with this state of being one with the universe. Some people call it sin, others lack of virtue, but it seems easier to be on a universal plane with the Spirit when your conscience is clear from anything that you feel in your core to be wrong. I am taught that we are born filthy and it is God's grace that makes us clean. I am in alignment with this, but it doesn't rid me of the responsibility to seek purity on a level that makes me accepting (not worthy) of God's grace. In essence, I believe God's grace is granted to us because—and only because—we believe, but seeking community with the Holy Spirit and the universe he commands is far easier when the energy you possess is free of guilt, free of the burden of negative energy. Remember guilt is a negative thought, if negative thoughts surround you then achieving a meditative state on a spiritual realm is very difficult, if not impossible.

Again, you don't have to be of my faith to believe that the universe offers this grace, and you can achieve it if you are of pure mind and body, even for a short period of time. The Holy Spirit doesn't wear a watch. Whether you want to admit it or not, you have the Spirit and you know down deep inside that when the fire of life is extinguished from your body, your soul will live on in the universe and allow believers like me to harness the power of the things in you that were good.

As you journey into achieving a meditative state, it isn't about seeking community with God, which is slightly more challenging. It is about seeking peace with the present, and setting the table if you will for a meal or a cup of coffee with Him. Put another way, you don't ask him to come to you, you invite the Holy Spirit to be within you. Thanking God (or the universe if you are a non-believer) for the things that He provides you is one of the most important steps. Humbly asking for peace to surround you, and trying to internalize all that you feel is the only way to reach this spiritually meditative state.

As you find yourself wandering off into a different train of thought, just gently stop yourself, clear your mind and begin again the process of being gracious for the gifts you have received.

To try and simplify this process for you, I will give you the 4 steps that have helped me. I find meditation to be very personal, so I was hesitant to list anything and instead ask you to do your own research on this, but since this is something you would have likely found anyway, I'll offer it here:

Step 1—Take 3 deep breaths where you use your diaphragm to bring air in and push air out. Try not to breathe shallowly; these are full slow breaths (it shouldn't make a bunch of noise, but it should sound more intense)

Step 2—Focus all of your attention on the present. Be mindful of the peacefulness of that present moment and begin the process of thanking the Holy Spirit for all that you have been given.

Step 3—Beginning with your feet, try and relax every muscle and tendon to make sure you feel comfortable. Start from the bottom up and focus on each body part in this order:

- Feet
- Ankles
- Calves
- Knees
- Quads
- Hips
- Lower back and lower abdomen
- Upper back and chest
- Shoulders
- Arms
- Neck
- Head

As you travel up the body, envision an energy field or aura that surrounds those parts and accept that the energy field is peaceful and its intent is to help you find your center and be in communion with the Holy Spirit.

Step 4—Once you have relaxed these parts of your body, be thankful for the gift of each and release anything that is nagging you from a pain perspective to that energy field that surrounds you. At this point you should be in a very peaceful state, try and remain in that moment and invite the Holy Spirit to be present and sit with you. If you are a non-believer you can ask that the universe to open its arms and be in communion with you. As you exit meditation, take three breaths again, but as you release them imagine that any negativity is leaving, carried away with every breath that leaves your body. Remember, be patient with this process and practice, practice, practice!

Humility—Okay, honesty alert. This one is tough for me. Humility is a virtue that I find extremely desirable and one that is very difficult for me at times. It is also the root of most of my problems. Humility is liberating and awesome, but sometimes to me displays itself in my mind's eye as weakness, and Joseph (my core) will have none of that. Obviously this is evil once again filling my head with things that are completely untrue. Merriam-Webster defines humility as 'being in the quality or state of not thinking you are better than other people.' I do not have an issue with thinking I am better than other people, but there are times that the words I choose may make it sound as if I do. I also place an extremely high value on execution and winning. I am not a believer that everyone wins. Participation trophies do not exist in my house. So there must be a winner and a loser, and sometimes my fervor for the 'W' makes it far too crowded for humility to live comfortably. So how do Type 'A' or 'win-at-all-cost' type guys and gals like me find a way to let humility reign supreme and invite the Spirit into their lives? Great question, and instead of suggesting that I know something more than you about this right after admitting that I have my own issues, I will take the liberty to point towards an individual that has all the reason in the world to say, "look at how GOOD I am!"

"Humility is the mother of all virtues; purity, charity and obedience. It is in being humble that our love becomes real, devoted and ardent. If you are humble nothing will touch you, neither praise nor disgrace, because you know what you are. If you are blamed you will not be discouraged. If they call you a saint you will not put yourself on a pedestal."
—Blessed Teresa of Calcutta

Better known to most as Mother Teresa, the great mother was the embodiment of humility and fully understood its power and how to harness the Holy Spirit. She felt so strongly about this she made a list that she called the 'Humility List.'

MOTHER TERESA'S HUMILITY LIST
1. Speak as little as possible about yourself.
2. Keep busy with your own affairs and not those of others.
3. Avoid curiosity.
4. Do not interfere in the affairs of others.
5. Accept small irritations with good humor.
6. Do not dwell on the faults of others.
7. Accept censures even if unmerited.
8. Give in to the will of others.
9. Accept insults and injuries.
10. Accept contempt, being forgotten and disregarded.
11. Be courteous and delicate even when provoked by someone.
12. Do not seek to be admired and loved.

Now, I often say as I stumble through life at times—making every mistake possible as if it were the goal—I remember that God asked us to be Christ *like*, not Christ, and I would say the same holds true here. I can set these virtues of humility as goals and strive to be more like Mother Teresa, but many of these things are far more difficult to do than it might seem. My suggestion is to start out small, and as you practice humility, it does get easier. Of course, saying you are good at humility isn't really the idea, now is it? Regardless, in the practical sense, practice these three concepts that are part of Mother Teresa's list, and humility will become easier to obtain.

1. Take responsibility for your misgivings that cause strife, and apologize with an admonishment to do better.

2. Accept daily irritations with good humor.

3. Be courteous and delicate, even when provoked.

Now, I have to say that this really does fly in the face of my 'ghetto' side. Now to be clear, I didn't live in the ghetto, but Joseph—my core—did, and he helps me to understand that humility doesn't have to be weak. Joseph and others, who are strong in will and stand up to fight when others cower, do so when it is virtuous, when we are fighting for the weak. When we are head to head with evil, our calling is one of protection. Mother Teresa's calling was one of love and acceptance, and she gave of herself in a manner that seemed effortless, and for her, maybe it was. Again, I am not asking you to be Mother Teresa, you will fail at this. I am asking you to learn from her approach, and try to practice the 3 items mentioned above to increase your ability to become humble. The payment for this effort is an alignment with your Spirit and the universe to a level you never thought possible. In order to summarize, the three key ways to help bring forth humility in your life are as follows: be courteous, take responsibility for the things you have done wrong, and handle irritants with humor and not hate.

You could also look at this by thinking about how evil would have you behave. It would be the exact opposite of these three keys to humility. It stands to reason that putting these in practice will bring forth more of the positive side of the universe than the negative. Do not fight evil, lest evil is oppressing the weak, then stand boldly and make it known that you are intolerant of bullying.

Improve the Connection

While my core is Joseph the strong warrior, I see my soul, which in my mind is the supernatural manifestation result of receiving the Holy Spirit, as a child that needs protection. When I am nearest to the Holy Spirit, I see an image of a young Jesus who has the knowledge of God, the curiosity of a child, and the wisdom of a cleric. This doesn't always occur in my prayers or in deep meditation, success at making the connection, in fact is fleeting at times. In order to get access to this perfect trifecta, I must strengthen my connection to it. Just like recreating the neuropathic access to muscles after surgery or an accident—any event that has forced us to execute some array of rehabilitation—we must work those pathways to gain access to the Spirit. This should be a main goal of your meditation! There are many ways to help strengthen this connection, and practicing the first two of these three steps that I am about to share will help you achieve the third. You must be deliberate about strengthening the connections, not just with your Soul and the Spirit (which is the appropriate place to start), but your mind and body. The key word in helping you to strengthen this connection is 'why.' Why do I feel this way about this person? Why does my body feel weak and lethargic today? Gaining a better understanding of the reasons behind our mental, physical and emotional state is an extremely important step on our way to reaching a higher state of optimal performance.

In essence, knowing why the car is not running well is 85% of the battle. If we know that, we will know what type of mechanic to take it to. So what must we do to strengthen the connection with the Holy Spirit and your soul? Let's ponder these steps.

1. Define what the Spirit is to you — I have a very strong faith and my thoughts of the Spirt is that of the Holy Spirt, part of the Trinity, but that doesn't mean that the Spirit can't manifest itself within me as 'my' soul! This is important, because you must know what you believe the Spirit is to you. To me, the Spirit is both external and internal. To clarify once again, I see the Holy Spirit as something outside of me that I can access through prayer, meditation and seeking community with daily. The soul is the manifestation of my supernatural spiritual core. In fact, for me I believe it has physical properties, only ones we can't detect on an MRI or XRAY; my spirit is the 'output' of my soul that has been nourished through my efforts with the Holy Spirit. Simply stated, your soul is what God has given you as the driver of your spirit, mind and body!

I have absolutely no data to prove that the soul has a physical weight or presence within my body, but I believe that it does. Keep in mind that I am not arguing that it does, I am merely saying that I believe it does, which helps me to access and utilize it when called upon. My feeble, prehistoric little mind sometimes needs to place things in the physical realm in order to utilize them, so to me the soul is physical within me and throughout me.

If you find this hard to swallow and need data or proof, I offer you this. If you have ever lost a father or a mother, or someone else close to you, your soul hurts! Not your emotions or your mind, your very core hurts, and for me at least, it is all the proof that I need. It is my assertion that physical pain in the center of your body can only be felt by physical things, hence my soul cries out in a very physical way, and that pain is proof that it physically exists.

Callie Joubert, in *Answers in Genesis*, writes extensively about the difference between the body and the soul, and points to numerous passages within the bible that give us a glimpse into what the relationship of the soul and the body must be in order to sustain life. Dr. Joubert's summation on this topic is spectacular, in that it explains that the soul to the body is very much like God is to the world; present but not physical. While this is at odds with my assertion that the soul has physical properties, Joubert goes on to surmise that the Soul 'is' the body, in that it is present everywhere within and throughout. So, I would argue that if this is true, is it not physical? Regardless of your thoughts here, and not to get hung up on this detail, the more important concept wouldn't be asking if the soul is physical, but instead, is your soul and its output, your spirit, in a healthy state.

Seek to understand what your version of the Holy Spirit looks like, and invite him to nourish your soul, creating a spiritual character that is in total alignment with what you were meant to do and be. Keep in mind, the soul, which I believe physically resides in your body, will cross over to the next life and I would suggest that our time on earth is necessary for our soul to get to the paradise that God has promised for those who believe. This would suggest that conditioning the soul today will make for a much easier transition to the next life.

2. Give the Spirit a physical manifestation in your mind — As I mentioned before, the more we give physical properties to the things that are not visible, the better defined and more easily accessible they become to us. The Holy Spirit has a very specific physical manifestation for me, I am positive it was placed there over the years of my Catholic, Christian upbringing. God, within my mind, is a regal entity in a flowing robe sitting on a throne with Jesus at his right hand. Wondering where that image came from? If you are not sure look up, "The Apostles Creed." Surrounding both God and Jesus is a shroud of light that engulfs the entire scene in my mind, and at the top is a white dove whose feathers surround God and Jesus in a protective blanket that is beautifully soft and seems to have life like a flowing stream. When I call on the Holy Spirit during prayer, the image never changes, but when I seek communion with the Holy Spirit, the image changes to the childlike Jesus that I mentioned earlier, and sits next to me to help mold and shape my soul. It is likely that I find this image less intimidating and it seems easier for me to ask for the help and knowledge of an all-knowing child.

Again, this is how I choose to physically imagine the Holy Spirit, and this may not be how you see it, but seeing it is the key. Decide how you see it and when you call on the spirit, access those mental images as if they are real. Draw it or write it down. These tasks will help your mind solidify the image and make it more accessible during meditation.

3. Engage the Spirit daily — Lastly, do this on a daily basis if you can. I am a martial arts instructor, and for 6 years of my life, I prepared fighters to enter various MMA tournaments. We used to say that the only way to learn how to fight is to fight, the same holds true here. To get good at this you have to do it... a lot! You will suck at this for a long time, but the clearer those images become in your mind's eye, the easier it will become. Meditation is a learned process and you do get better the more that you do it. You will find creative ways to fit this into your day and if you put your mind to it and use the steps given earlier in this chapter, engaging the Holy Spirit daily becomes a very rewarding experience.

Continual improvement of this state — A general rule of thumb is to aggressively seek the Spirit 4 times per week, but at least for the first year, daily is much better! Some people need to do it every day to make any progress. Once you have reached this sense of communion with the Holy Spirit, you will always want to come back and do it again. Sadly, you will find that the same result does not occur all the time and it has to do with the condition of mind and body, and all that is around you. Be patient and understand that every attempt at accessing the Spirit in meditation is still a positive experience for your body, but when you really connect and find that you are sitting with the Spirit and receive nourishment from that Spirit, you will be forever hooked on the desire to do it again.

Author's note –

Without a doubt, this chapter was the hardest to write. I struggled through it for various reasons, some were health related and some were related to motivation. I am telling you this because I am not one to shirk my responsibilities, and I rarely get sick. Motivation for me has never been an issue, and suddenly as I began to delve deep into my spirit and put those revelations on paper, I found myself in a deep state of depression.

I had thoughts about stopping this writing all-together, and continued to ask myself, who I thought I was and why I thought I could help anyone with this book. In my opinion, this onslaught of health issues and attacks to my motivation and confidence cannot be a co-incidence. I am writing about the good of the Holy Spirit. If you think that maybe, just maybe, I got the attention of evil, and that those thoughts were being placed in my head to get me to stop, I would have to agree with you.

For the record, this experience has strengthened my resolve to finish! It is obvious to me that the negative forces at work around us exist, and for some reason it does not want this book written. This fact alone makes me want to persevere and find a way to get this in front of the many people who seek out advice. I am looking forward to sharing this with my children and maybe the world and the negativity that surrounds us will just have to be that spectator again looking on with disgust! If this publication helps one person, then I have a lasting legacy impression with that person and for me, that is enough to make it all worth it.

CHAPTER 4

Mind

"There are no constraints on the human mind,
no walls around the human spirit, no barriers to our progress
except those we ourselves erect."
—Ronald Reagan

MR. REAGAN WAS disliked by few people and could bring the two parties of government together better than any other President in the recent past. It is statements like the one quoted here that give us a glimpse inside a man who likely already knew many of the things that we still try to understand every day.

I recognize that this may be one of those chapters that you may have to go back and read again. I will make a number of conclusions in my findings when speaking about the brain and the mindfulness that it creates. It may be advantageous to use a highlighter or take notes as you read this chapter. I have also italicized and bolded certain sentences that are more important concepts to understand. As you read you will see that many of my hypotheses build on one another. The conclusions, hypothesis and thought provoking positions that I take in this chapter are meant to create one thing, the thought or suggestion that the brain and our body is an engine that helps us produce mindfulness. It isn't mindfulness itself.

While the soul and the supernatural spirit that you possess

should be creating the perfect environment for the rest of our core components to interact within, the mind is the part of our existence that creates the plan and logically executes said plan throughout our lives.

Incidentally, why is it easy for us to accept that the 'mind' comes from the organ called our brain, but it is so difficult to believe that our soul comes from any organ in the body at all? The brain doesn't 'produce' mindfulness; this is achieved through our brain and the rest of our senses working cohesively to form a heightened sense of consciousness. Why then do we struggle with the thought that all or any of our senses are involved in the existence of our soul? I would ask you to contemplate this thought during meditation, and if you have a clear answer let me know. I would be interested to hear your take on the matter.

The concept of the 'mind' is no more real or tangible than that of the soul. Those of you, who doubt that your soul exists, may want to think about whether your mind is real as well. We have no proof that your brain truly is the keeper of the mind, but we seem to broadly and blindly accept this notion. Why then is the soul such a stretch for so many? While I am digressing and mixing the concepts of the soul and the mind, I would say to the sceptics that struggle with the existence of the soul, to only consider this oversimplification. If the brain can create an intangible thing called the 'mind' why then can the heart or surrounding senses not create the intangible thing called the soul? While you contemplate this notion, let's get back to the "mind" and how our bodies create the state of mindfulness.

I would assert to you based on the various research I have done and the research of others that I have carefully studied, that the *mind* is powered by the brain, and mindfulness can only be achieved through awareness, consciousness and interaction with our world.

This suggests there is a big difference between the brain that carries out automatic and manual processes of thought, and the mind that interacts with our spirit and our body, and creates the concept of mindfulness.

In an article published in *The Best Brain Possible* with Debbie Hampton, this question was posed to Dr. Daniel Siegel, a professor of psychiatry at UCLA school of Medicine, co-director of the UCLA Mindfulness Awareness Research Center. As the executive director of the Mindsight Institute, and author of several books, he coined a concept called 'Mindsight,' and utilized this notion to describe the human capacity to perceive the mind of the self and others.

It is a common belief that the mind is the activity of the brain. He proposes that this is only one part of it.

In Chapter 1, we spoke of finding our center, or our core. Looking to ancient eastern philosophies and practices, we discussed Qi and surmised that finding the center was finding 'well-being.' Dr. Siegel's approach to the concept of well-being is as much about the mind as it is the soul. He calls this the 'Triangle of Well-Being' and his assertions are completely in line with my research and practice of what many believe to be mindfulness.

On the Triangle of Well-Being, each point of the triangle is an essential component of mental health. One point is the physical brain and nervous system which are the mechanisms by which energy and information flow throughout our beings. Our senses take in information from the environment. These become electrical signals which travel through the nervous system to the brain, then, a response of neurochemicals and electrical signals regulate the body, control movement and influence emotions.

A second point on the Triangle of Well-Being is relationships, which are the means by which information and energy are shared. An integral part of the mind is comprised of the relational process of energy and information flowing between and among people. This happens through the spoken or written word. In person, this also happens through eye contact, facial expression, body language, posture and gesture. In the previous chapter, we spoke of the importance of community with the Holy Spirit; it seems with regard to mindfulness, the same holds true for relationships with others as well.

The third point on the *Triangle of Well-Being* is the mind, and mental health can be achieved only if all of these points are tended to by your consciousness.

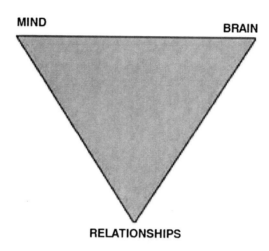

In his book, _Mindsight: The New Science of Personal Transformation,_ he writes:

"Our minds are created within relationships – including the one that we have with ourselves... Each of us has a unique mind: unique thoughts, feelings, perceptions, memories, beliefs, and attitudes, and a unique set of regulatory patterns. These patterns shape the flow of energy and information inside us, and we share them with other minds."

The mind controls the motor functions of the body, no doubt, but as we study Dr. Siegel's work, we find that mental health is far more complex and relationships are needed in order to remain healthy. I would suggest that this mindfulness only exists when you can share your conscious life with someone with whom you have a relationship. This person or group of persons do not have to be those of intimate relationships, it can be friends, relatives or if you are fortunate enough to have a spouse that you still like and want to be around—I digress a bit. Anyway, if you have relationships, you have the beginnings of a healthy mind.

Mental health, optimal performance and becoming the best version of you, starts with building a spiritual foundation. We do this by inviting the Holy Spirit to have a relationship with us. To nurture the mind, we have to do the same with the people we love here on earth. Why do suicide rates go up during the holidays? Because the mental clarity that we seek only comes when we have relationships that can help provide the back drop necessary to achieve clarity of life and purpose (the why) which as we know can lead to fulfillment. The holidays make us hyper-focused on the failures of those relationships, or the fact that there are no relationships at all. This leaves many individuals feeling as if their lives have no meaning, no purpose and therefore, the feeling that they are already dead. By the way, I have stated that death is "beautiful," due to the fact that it is the crossing of our soul to the supernatural realm or in my belief, heaven. With respect to suicide, it is evil winning and there is nothing beautiful about that!

Keep in mind we are searching for the most optimal version of ourselves and a practical approach on how to get there, the ability to approach everything in an *Enhanced* manner! What we should already be accepting is that trying to do this by ourselves or having no one to share that experience with makes it nearly impossible to achieve.

Mindfulness is essential to allow the three core components to work in unison, and mindfulness needs relationships with people here on earth in order to make the triangle complete.

Relationships are food for the mind. Seek first, your relationship with the Holy Spirit as detailed in Chapter 3, and all of your other relationships will be much more meaningful.

The Brain

It is difficult to talk about mindfulness without discussing the role that the brain plays in all of this. The brain/mind debate can be a long and drawn out discussion. What we must concede is that our brain carries out many tasks within our body without a hint of 'mindfulness.'

It is no accident that we speak of spirit, mind, body rather than spirit, brain, body. The spirit does not interact with the brain, it interacts with the mind, and if we are true to allowing the spirit to drive, it is the mind that is the passenger and the brain is simply a component of the car. It goes without saying that the brain is an incredibly important component organ and without brain activity you could argue that we have no consciousness, but we have no proof that our mindfulness does not live on, even when our brain ceases to show activity.

That being said, anyone who has ever had a panic attack knows that no matter what the "mindful" side of your body wants to do, the prehistoric brain will sometimes garner control over the mind. This shows the power that the brain has over the body, and if mindfulness does not exist we sometimes become victim to it. Many people who suffer from mental instability issues have an overactive prehistoric portion of the brain and rarely exist in a mindful state.

I will use public speaking as an example. As I have gotten older, it seems as if my brain wants my body to believe that public speaking (something I love to do) is some sort of life or death emergency. One of the worst things ever to happen to someone who speaks in front of people happened to me! I had a full on panic attack and had to excuse myself to regain my composure. My brain was taking over the body, and my mindfulness couldn't talk the brain out of it once it started. Since I truly am a biohacker, I started looking at the body and my nutrition regimen first for clues as to why this happened. There were numerous causes that day that included stress, higher than normal cortisol levels, and well, the 4 cups of coffee obviously didn't help. Proof that nutrition impacts the body, but we will speak to that in the next chapter. One simple thing I did to help curb my bodies desire for me to fight when my adrenaline begins to flow, is to simply write down on my presentation notes, 'You will not be fighting today,' and 'There is no emergency.' These two simple phrases have helped me to allow my mind to have dominion over my body, instead of allowing my prehistoric brain to take over.

At this point of our discussion, I must admit that while I have done an enormous amount of research on the brain and its activities, I am not a doctor or neuropsychologist that can discuss with you the specifics of the central nervous system, or how the brain works in any detail. In fact, I fought the desire to go into a long diatribe about how the brain works, quoting many doctors and neuro psychologists in this section. With all of that being said, there are some basic things that we need to understand about the brain so we are equipped with what it takes to allow the mind to have control.

Brain basics

There are various areas of the brain and of course those areas control very specific things such as sight, smell, taste, etc., which can lead to awareness, but not necessarily consciousness, and definitely not mindfulness. We will have more on this a little later. The ironic thing is that the only thing that the brain has that resembles something of mindfulness is 'body awareness.' Your brain is aware of your body and this further explains how the spirit, mind, body connection can be made - *because the core components of the brain functions with body awareness. If you are successful at allowing the spirit dominion over your mind, and the body truly is in a shroud of the soul, it stands to reason that the brain is aware of all contents of the body, including the soul.* This basically means that not only can the brain see the soul, it wants to be in alignment with it. Incidentally, so does your mind and when you get them working as one, you can then make the final step of incorporating the body and placing it in parallel with the mind and the spirit. This is when we achieve the heightened experience of hyper-consciousness and extreme sensory awareness of our surroundings!

Neuroplasticity – The concept to understand when we speak of the brain is that there are neuro-pathways that are created when we teach the brain to think in a certain way. These pathways become small programs in the brain that are basically 'If, then' statements. If this happens, then do this. These pathways can be very positive and sometimes very negative. As I mentioned about my public speaking issue, my brain had created a pathway that said: "If adrenaline shows up, then trigger the fight or flight response mechanism." This obviously is not a situation where I needed to do either one. You guys know that Joseph (my core) would do anything to protect my soul, which as we have discussed radiates throughout my body, but I don't need Joseph in this situation. I just need to calmly and passionately deliver my presentation, nothing more. The first thing I needed to do was to alter this program and remove the fight or flight response from this activity. This is possible because of the brains ability to change these little programs. This is neuroplasticity at work.

We speak of the soul as the immortal part of the body that lives on, allowing the spirit dominion over the mind, and your mindfulness—and dare I say consciousness—get to ride along to immortality. This truly is the meaning of the afterlife, and if both of these components are healthy, then we have set ourselves up for a great life on earth and after, as we promised in the introduction of this text.

Going back to Merriam-Webster, mindfulness is defined as: the practice of maintaining a nonjudgmental state of heightened or complete awareness of one's thoughts, emotions, or experiences on a moment-to-moment basis.

I find it ironic that even Webster struggles to suggest that mindfulness comes from the brain. *Could it be that the soul engulfs the body and is of the body, and could consequently also be responsible for mindfulness?* Where does that leave the brain? It seems as if the brain is a very complex power source, carrying out numerous functions and facilitating the mindfulness that we enjoy each day. *In essence, the brain is the calculator carrying out the equations of life, but I am finding more and more that true mindfulness and consciousness is a product of the soul.*

Let's take this one step further and really blow your mind. Okay, maybe a bad choice of words here. Is it possible that consciousness is comparable to the notion that God is, was and always will be? Let me say that a different way. *Is it possible that our consciousness and our soul always was, and we were unaware of it until such time at birth, when our brain was capable of processing that with which the mind or our consciousness had already begun to engage in before we came to know this plane of existence? In essence, is consciousness recognizable to humans because the brain powers our awareness and we can now perceive it?* Was consciousness always there just waiting for a vessel to ride in and we were not 'aware' of it? Does this mean that after our death, our soul and our consciousness will remain because our brain was nothing more than the power source and central processing unit we needed to begin the journey of awareness? *If that is true, then what, after death, shall we say 'powers' and processes mindfulness so that our consciousness can exist?* I would suggest to you that if you follow this program and get your core components in alignment you will know the answer because utilization of the supernatural power of the Holy Spirit is unmistakable and if you tap into that power you will understand what it is like to live "Enhanced!" You can use the power of the brain, but the Holy Spirit's power is limitless. After death; therefore, It is the power that the Holy Spirit provides, the energy to allow consciousness and His power and pure energy is so remarkable that the level of consciousness and the knowledge obtained by the soul crossing over are immeasurable and far from our understanding today. In essence, our brain, central nervous system and heart provide a fairly efficient power or life source, but we have to work to connect to the rest of the Universe and the Holy Spirit to have a heightened experience of life on earth. When we cross, we will become of the Spirit or the Universe and we will know of all He knows. Make no mistake, I am not saying we will become deity, but we will have a pure connection with the Holy Spirit and be conscious of how deity, if you will, behaves. We will be in constant contact and communion with the Holy Spirit and this is why we should all see the passing of a loved one as a wonderful opportunity for their soul, even though we will miss them on earth.

In 1 Corinthians 15:51-57 we read: *"Behold! I tell you a mystery. We shall not all sleep, but we shall all be changed, in a moment, in the twinkling of an eye, at the last trumpet. For the trumpet will sound, and the dead will be raised imperishable, and we shall be changed. For this perishable body must put on the imperishable, and this mortal body must put on immortality. When the perishable puts on the imperishable, and the mortal puts on immortality, then shall come to pass the saying that is written: 'Death is swallowed up in victory. O death, where is your victory? O death, where is your sting?'"*

This verse has always spoken to me, saying that we go through a complete change as we cross over after death. We become 'imperishable.' In Corinthians, it is described as putting on a garment of immortality. If we are to speak of immortality with such literalism, why would it be so hard to believe that our consciousness would not travel with our spirit to be back to the source of the power given to us on earth?

Earlier in the 2 Corinthians Chapter 5:8, we read: *"Yes, we are of good courage, and we would rather be away from the body and at home with the Lord."*

This clears it up for me that we will be away from the body but connected and 'home' with the powerful source that breathed air into our lungs in the beginning of our earthly journey. The only way to be "home" is to return to a place that once was considered that. This suggests to me that being one with the Holy Spirit is a state that has happened before and supports my theory that we are conscious of life because our Body and Mind are allowing us to be, but the natural state for us to return is oneness with the Holy Spirit. I believe this soul that we have is what makes us the chosen, and to ignore it, is like buying a 1968 Ford Mustang Shelby GT and never driving it… I digress but with about 400 horse power no less! So why must we go through this earthly phase? This takes us back to God's promise to us of freewill! We must live through this life on earth to choose him without His influence thrust upon us. We can seek His influence and He will provide it, but we must seek it out! This is where most organized Religions get it wrong. We are not on this earth to prove to God that we are worthy to be in heaven. We are on Earth so we can decide if going back home is what we want!

More about our brain

Returning to the here and now and our time on earth, we have to continue to utilize this vessel to execute our daily tasks and do what we can to allow our consciousness and mindfulness to create the life and outcomes that we wish.

Another theory might be that consciousness is nothing more than the sum total of the brain's output, but what of people who lay comatose only to wake up and remember many things that were going on around them. This would suggest that mindfulness or consciousness is controlled not just in the brain, but also within other areas of the body.

Dr. Billy Gordon stated in an article in *Psychology Today,* that the brain is a "tangible organ in the body that controls all vital human functions. Conversely the mind permeates every cell of the human body." He goes on to say that, "more importantly, the mind ultimately has dominion over the brain."

I find it interesting that we have said that the Holy Spirit impacts your soul and your spiritual nature should be allowed dominion over your logical mind, and also that the soul is found throughout the body. Here **Dr. Gordon is saying that the mind permeates every cell.** This makes the process of the soul having dominion over the mind not so difficult to understand and very plausible. *Also, if the mind has dominion over the brain, and the brain controls all vital human functions, is it not fair to concede that your spirit can truly impact your body physically.*

Again, we can extrapolate that the spiritual connection with the universe or the Holy Spirit can have a real physical effect on the body. This could truly explain the many well documented miracles of healing that we hear of today. If the spirit can have dominion and therefore regulate the mind, and the mind can have dominion and therefore regulate the body, spiritual healing does not seem so far-fetched. Miracles become much easier to explain if we had a deeper connection with the concepts of universal metaphysical control.

When science tries to explain something away so profusely that smart people begin to use stupid hypothesis, it typically raises a flag for me. Most scientists cannot accept occurrences as being "of the Holy Spirit," so often times the research removes the findings that do not support an explanation of this world. Don't fall for the notion that there is no proof of the spiritual realm and its ability to supersede that of the physical.

I feel as though we have made a strong case for the mind, which is powered by, but has dominion over the body and that it truly is present in every cell. Remember though, that what originates from one thing often tries to mimic its maker. Often times we 'act' like our parents, sometimes our mind will try and 'act' like a brain which is nothing more than a processor of information with no forethought of the consequences. Sometimes when we are endeavoring to be 'logical' we end up becoming callas or dispirited in our approach because we are choosing to use the "brain" - instead of the mind - in a mindful task. This often forces us down a path of pure logic and not down the path of love or humility which never ends with fulfillment of the heart and soul.

We were created to be in alignment with the Holy Spirit and therefore the universe.

It has been said that being in proper alignment is called 'walking in the spirit,' while being out of alignment is called 'walking in the flesh.' This concept supports the notions that we are proposing and goes one step further. We have been trying to explain how to 'walk in the spirit' through the process of engaging the spirit and the mind. Since both emanate throughout the body, with focused effort we should be able to do this, but what if we don't? If we don't, we will walk in the flesh only and the connection to the rest of the world is severed. Our bodily vessel is a complex array of carbon, organs, tissue and water. Without a connection to the universe, it will become nothing more than what each individual part can achieve. The heart will pump your blood, your brain will process information and the muscles will contract. In essence you become a complex machine that operates more robotically than spiritually. Connect that machine to the Holy Spirit and the universe, and what you can achieve becomes far more spectacular and rewarding.

So how do we control the mind?

In order to control the mind, we need to delve deeper into how we react to things within and around us. There are three phases that we go through when the mind begins to interact with its surroundings. The first phase is awareness.

Awareness – The mind is aware because it utilizes its 5 senses to place it in this state of awareness. Factors like sensations, smells, tastes and something as abstract as perceptions all work with the mind to accomplish this.

Consciousness – Awareness must exist before we can be conscious of it. Consciousness takes the awareness to a different level. It begins to play out how your spirit, mind, and body might choose to interact with what you have become aware of. For instance, you might say that I am now aware that my wife is home from work, so I am going to greet her, kiss her and ask her how her day went. This is the deliberate thought of what you might do about the awareness. The final phase is integration.

Integration - Integration is the executing of the plans made by the conscious mind to interact or integrate with the thing that you were made aware of.

These three steps that the brain and mind go through happen almost instantly dependent upon the situation. There are often times that we skip all of these steps and our brain just reacts. There is no mindfulness in our body's fight or flight response. The brain just sends the signal to either take a swing or run like hell. Now that we have a clearer picture of the role that mindfulness and the brain play in our quest to have an extraordinary life, it is time to answer the question practically of what do we do to put the brain and our mind in the best position to impact the body and work in unison with the other two core components?

Remember, the brain can orchestrate certain functions of the body, but the mind can impact all of them. As we go through the next section, look at the minds job as not just the ability to work with the brain to impact the body internally, the mind can also impact what is external to the body and help bring it within. Since this could be both good and bad external sources of energy as we discussed in the previous chapters, knowing how to set the mind on the proper path of engagement is crucial to achieving the extraordinary person that we wish to be.

Understanding that the three phases that mindfulness goes through to create a moment in existence, we are better prepared to place the mind in the best position for success. We must understand that we are first aware of a concept, then conscious that this concept can impact us. Then we begin to think about how that might occur, and finally, acting on that plan through engagement and integration, allows at the very least to better understand how existence turns into integration with our surroundings.

> **"Don't just look, observe. Don't just swallow, taste. Don't just sleep, dream. Don't just think, feel. Don't just exist, LIVE."**
> **— Unknown**

These simple suggestions will give you some insight into our next discussion points. Life is too rich to just be a spectator. We must engage life, and more importantly, engage others that are living in a positive state of mind, helping those that are not, in order to obtain the wealth of fulfillment. Creating a legacy must come one legacy impression at a time. In order to do this we must have our core components—spirit, mind, and body—all working in unison, and the key to doing all of this as suggested by Dr. Daniel Siegel, is relationships.

How relationships impact mindfulness can best be described utilizing a concept first proposed by Aristotle, the notion of 'the whole is greater than the sum of the parts.'

In essence, individually we can accomplish certain things, but through relationships and fostering the mental health that relationships create, allow 1 + 1 to suddenly equal 3. Why does this happen? Because the connection with the universe becomes much stronger! We are all of the same frequency if we are all in a positive state. Surround yourself with and seek to engage in community with these people and you will find life becoming much richer, obstacles to happiness fewer and much easier to overcome. This is why it is important also to take care when approaching the negative person. A negative relationship can equal '3' as well, just in the opposite direction. With Newton's first law of motion at work here, once you start moving in that direction, it is difficult to stop and turn it around. In this case, if 1 + 1 equals 3 in the negative, the outcome can become exponentially worse. This could explain why abusive relationships tend to ruin everything else for that person as they experience the worst of the relationship.

So our focus as we work to improve the connection with the mind should be as follows:

1. Accept what mindfulness is and work to understand how we can impact every function of the brain. After all, it is your brain!

2. Accept that the Holy Spirit or the universe has dominion over your soul and spirit, and that your spirit should be allowed dominion over the mind.

3. Accept that relationships are the key to nourish and enhance your mindfulness experience, placing you squarely in the

middle of the positive or negative energy of the universe.

It may be worth noting something again that I mentioned previously.

I am a believer in the Holy Spirit, and I believe that the Holy Spirit has dominion over the universe. I believe that the universe and the Holy Spirit are two distinctly different things. You will see me speaking of these two different things sometimes as one. I do this to reach out to those who are troubled with the thought of a Holy Spirit. I don't do this to propose that they are correct, but to expose them to the notion that if they can believe that the universe exists and it has extraordinary power, so too can the Holy Spirit. Am I trying to convert non-believers into believing in one God that commands all? The simple answer—and to be completely transparent—is… ABSOLUTELY! If this troubles you, stop reading! My attempts won't be overt, but my logic will make you question if I just might be on to something.

Back to the 3 phases

Awareness – There is little we need to do to place the brain and the mind in the best position to execute awareness… our body handles this for us

Consciousness – This takes a little more deliberate planning, and if we have allowed the spirit dominion over the mind and we have a strong bond with the universe, the planning part of consciousness becomes far easier and we gain alignment quickly.

Integration – In this world nothing is real until we act, our integration with the stimulus or situation that the brain was handed will be easy because consciousness gave us the plan. Our execution of that plan is crucial and this is where mindfulness truly resides. So what are the practical ways that we can integrate with our surroundings in a more enlightened way? Read on my friend, the keys to an extraordinary life are being laid before you and you may want to take some notes, because this is about to get real…

I digress a bit.

As we have been told since our baseball playing adolescent years, practice makes perfect. Sometimes you just can't refute parental wisdom. In the case of mindfulness, Mom and Dad had it right again. We can practice mindfulness and how to supercharge our integration with life by focusing on some very specific things. Our integration into the universe, relationships, and what seem to only be our mundane daily interactions is an extremely important process that we must master as if we were an Olympic athlete preparing for the games. When we are engaging and integrating extremely well, we are at the peak of universal power acceptance, I call this being in the Integration Zone or just the 'zone' for short. Many people speak of the zone in sport so it made sense to me, because the feeling seemed very similar to when I achieved a higher level of mindfulness for the first time. It was as if everything was in slow motion, and my thoughts were perfectly aligned with what the universe desired for me. As if my brain was aware of everything, my consciousness was laying down plans that could only be described as perfection, and my execution of integration was flawless. There is some science behind why this happens. I found the best description of this in the October 6th publishing of *The Mind Unleashed,* by Dr. Kelley Neff. She defines my 'zone' as 'the flow' and this concept is widely accepted by many scientists.

Dr. Kelly Neff is a social psychologist, author and educator, who has reached millions of people with her articles, radio show and website, The Lucid Planet.

She describes the following:

Brain Wave Transition — *While in a state of flow, our brainwaves transition from the more rapid beta waves of waking consciousness to slower alpha waves, and even to the border of much slower theta waves. Alpha waves are associated with relaxed and effortless alertness, peak performance and creativity, while theta waves are associated with the deeper dream-state consciousness and experienced predominately during REM sleep.*

Pre-Frontal Cortex Deactivation — *During flow states, the Pre-Frontal Cortex (PFC) becomes deactivated in a process called 'transient hypo-frontality.' The PFC is the area of the brain that houses higher-level cognitions, including those that help us to cultivate our ego and sense of self. During a flow state this area becomes deactivated, helping us lose ourselves in the task at hand and silence our criticisms, fears and self-doubts.*

Neuro-chemistry — *Flow states also trigger a release of many of the pleasurable and performance-inducing chemicals in the brain, including dopamine, serotonin, norepinephrine and endorphins. A recent study shows that when we are intrinsically curious about an outcome and driven for answers, dopamine is released in the brain, helping to solidify our memories. These findings suggest why flow states are good for promoting learning and memory in addition to creativity.*

So how do we utilize this to improve mindfulness?

I have developed these 7 steps over the years of trying to hone the state of extraordinary mindfulness, and this undoubtedly will help get you to a new state of mind and state of being.

1. Practice Focus
2. Develop a plan of integration for repetitive situations
   a. Introductions
   b. Meeting new people
   c. Delivering praise
   d. Delivering bad news
3. Meditation with a focus on mindfulness and being in the moment only (we will not engage the Holy Spirit here, He is already there)
4. Slow down!
5. Do something creative and interesting that tests your skills, this helps us to be 'present' in the moment

6. Seek out positive relationships and be in the moment when en-gaging those relationships.
7. Using Neuroplasticity to our advantage.

Practice Focus — Focus is not required to be aware, but is required to be mindful. Anything worth doing is worth practicing and we have learned through many scientific studies that we can exercise the brain through numerous phases of testing and rest, much like muscles react to interval training.

There are brain teaser games and apps available for your computer or smart phone that can help in this area and it allows the brain the ability to focus on a single task. Keep in mind these games are not quite the 'miracle app' they claim to be, but studies show they can be helpful.

Other helpful brain health activities were mentioned in an article written in *Live Science*, September 4th 2014, by John Swartzberg. He cites that, "The best brain-health advice, based largely on observational findings, is to lead a physically active, intellectually challenging and socially engaged life. In particular, much research shows that physical exercise is a moderately effective way to maintain, and even improve, brain fitness."

Obviously we will cover more on the above statement in the next chapter, "Body," but it is relevant to mention here as well.

Along with the potential of an app that helps you focus the mind, I find that utilizing 'focus practice' right before meditation is a great way to not just train the brain to move past awareness, but it also sets me up for a great meditation session.

In my house I have set up what I call my 'meditation station' which is nothing more than a small room with a really comfortable chair and an audio source that allows me to utilize guided meditation or just soft music to help me with my focus. For about 3 to 4 minutes I will take an object, a picture, or some other item that I can truly focus on prior to meditation. Recognizing all the details of this object forces my brain to pick up on things that I never noticed before. There are pictures in my house that I have walked past for years, and during my focus practice found that the pictures had things in them I had never seen. Not only does this allow me to train the brain to be more focused, it sets me up for a good meditation session, and it also proves to me that we can be aware of a picture that is in and around us daily, but never really be mindful of it. This is the description of most of our everyday lives. "Awareness of our life with no real appreciation or active engagement, due to only consciousness with no interaction or integration."

Develop a plan of Integration — Once you have honed your skills of focus and taken your awareness to a level of heightened consciousness, integration becomes easier. There are many different situations in life and having the appropriate response to each is not as easy as you think. In fact, most patients with psychiatric issues present symptoms of inappropriate responses to various situations. The unhealthy brain is still aware and may still be conscious, but it is the step of integration planning that is hindered. I would argue that roughly 25% of our integration planning is done automatically by our heightened level of consciousness, and then we depend on our mind to complete the integration plan in its entirety before we execute. This obviously happens quickly and often times we may size up a situation and only have one step in the plan.

For example, you may see a new face at a social event and surmise that the first step in the plan is to step forward and introduce yourself. Seems easy enough, right? Imagine the same interaction had your heightened consciousness informed your mindfulness during the integration plan that the new face was wearing a class ring from Wharton Business School. The conversation may change from, "Hi, my name is Don," to "Hi, I see you went to Wharton!" The conversation would be a bit richer and that integration would produce a much more intimate outcome.

So how do we practice this? In our marketing department at my systems integration company—Vista Information Systems— we used

to call this the 'sandwich.' In some advertisements you will see companies use the same introduction, the same ending and only the content changes. We see this now in websites and print advertising as
well. The bread is the beginning and the end, but the content is the
middle of the sandwich.

This can be utilized for what we would consider those common
interactions. Introductions, meeting new people, delivering praise or
bad news are all common interactions and more importantly integra-
tions with another person's mindfulness. This is where you can build
a short plan of what to be conscious of, and then put it into your
integration sandwich. As you become better at these more common
interactions, you will also notice that you become better at other interactions as well.

Trust that your heightened consciousness will speak to your mindfulness and then allow your core to shine through. I am a very outgo-
ing person and I love interactions with people. At some point in my
life's journey, I found that social anxiety began to creep into my life.
What was happening? After much reflection and meditation, I found
I was placing too much importance on what the other party thought
of the interaction with me. My ego was interfering with my integration plan, and was placing too much importance on that one event.
More importantly, I was worried more about myself than the moment
and the interaction. Relationships only bear fruit when both parties
are important, not just you. To further squelch my need for situational
acceptance, I had to remember that opinions are created over a cul-
mination of events, not one single exposure. Legacy is typically created through a lifetime of work, not a moment in time. While first
impressions are crucial, you can't tell your life's story in one chance
meeting. Sometimes it is good to leave a little for the next time. For
those with social anxiety, it is important to note that no one meeting
is nearly that important, it is the combined interactions that make you
who you are. Trust me, I have yet to meet someone and enter into a
real relationship where there wasn't something positive to pull from
it.

Meditation — This is an easy one, so I won't spend much time on it because we already have in other chapters. Meditation *is* mindfulness. Being in the moment is the core of meditation, and so is mindfulness. I have described the 'mindfulness zone' or as others call it 'the flow,' as a heightened consciously-aware, almost meditative state of mindfulness. Athletes are heard stating 'the game has slowed down for me.' What they mean is, it is much easier to execute because what used to be too fast to integrate with, has now slowed and the integration plans are much improved.

My coaches at Enhanced Sports Performance use this concept and ability to help athletes recognize and integrate quickly so they know just what to do with their God given athletic abilities in situations that are repetitive in their sport.

Concentrate and focus on mindfulness, and during your meditative sessions practice focus, and you will have this step licked!

Slow Down — Sometimes we have to slow down to go faster. Athletes break down their sport into smaller chunks so they can concentrate on every aspect. A basketball player may only work on jumping one day, and a baseball player may only work on his slide step before a throw to first base. Consider this for mindfulness as well. Slow down and allow your brain the ability to provide your mindfulness with good actionable data. Choose times during the day where you plan to be more mindful of your surroundings and your interactions. In the past as I have noticed my skills diminishing in this area, I have broken down the event or item where I am struggling most into compartmentalized sections so I can evaluate where I am having issues. For instance, I struggle at times with name and face recognition. In essence, I tend to introduce myself then forget the person's name minutes after he or she has just told me. After breaking this down, I found that I am typically too anxious to develop the relationship, so I end up missing the biggest step in the process, knowing the name of the person I am engaging. If I slow down and become truly mindful of the person that I am speaking with, forgetting his or her name is almost impossible.

If I notice that other areas of engagement are deteriorating, I may tell the individual that I am meeting with that I may have longer pauses today between sentences. Since this meeting and our interaction is extremely important to me, I want to hear their opinions and allow them to conjure thoughtfulness instead of planning my next answer or statement. It is amazing the response you get. Open mindedness becomes the goal of the meeting, and you may find a much more fruitful interaction.

Do something creative — There are numerous peer-reviewed scientific papers that prove mindfulness improves mental and physical well-being, while also enhancing creativity and decision making. I have found that the reverse is true as well. When we engage in the creative process we access many different areas of the brain. Sometimes this process takes us deeper than just awareness, consciousness and integration. In order to engage in the creative process, we must prepare to do so in a manner that differs slightly than that of conscious integration and makes the brain work in a little different way than the normal functions that we engage in daily. Chrystal Goh wrote in an article titled "How to Apply Mindfulness to the Creative Process," that there are four stages that we must go through in the creative process: Preparation, Incubation, Illumination and Verification.

As you can see, these are all areas that seem to suggest a more mindful approach to thought. You can't just be aware of creativity, you must engage. In essence, you can be aware of art in the room, but you must be engaged to create it.

Seek out Relationships — Dr. Siegel asserts that relationships are the means by which information is shared. Keep in mind this is a two way street and you want to make sure that the information you are providing, as well as receiving, is the information that supports the reality you wish to create. There are many relationships that are not good for us and we should quickly remove those from our lives. Your spirit can be negatively impacted by these relationships and we are starting to see why mindfulness controlled by our spirit is so crucial in achieving a life that is extraordinary. If your spirit is filled with negativity and has dominion over your mind and body then negative things are attracted to you.

Well known author Derek Rydell of the best-selling book *Emergence* states it best. "The things we want are already with us." In fact he asserts that if we are waiting on something, the truth is we already have it, it is likely waiting on us to set into motion the plans, activities and execution that it takes to have it.

A negative spirit will likely not create that environment unless negative things are what you want. Relationships should be sought out with care. We have spoken of our virtual sphere of influence. The physical sphere of influence includes relationships that should enhance your life, not detract from it.

Once in that positive relationship, utilize your mindfulness focus when interacting with them. Be 'fully' present. Fullness of the mind can only be achieved when we have fullness of the steps that it takes to get there. If you have taken good care and made good choices with your relationships, don't just listen, hear the meaning of the relationships you keep. Each one is precious and was placed there by your spirit to provide a nurturing of your soul. Integrating that person's knowledge, life experiences and spirit can enhance you just as it has him or her. This is why the relationships we create, and more importantly maintain, are so important.

Neuroplasticity — We could write an entire chapter on Neuroplasticity, which is defined by Medicine.net as the "brain's ability to reorganize itself by forming new neural connections throughout life. Neuroplasticity allows the neurons (nerve cells) in the brain to compensate for injury and disease, and to adjust their activities in response to new situations or to changes in their environment." The great news about neuroplasticity is we can change the way we think by creating new neuropathways through constant repetition and re-programming of the way we think. The main thing to consider here is that the same holds true for the negative self-talk that many engage in. If we tell ourselves that we are not worthy of receiving that which we want, then we will build neuropathways that can help to sabotage the very thing that we believe we want. Stopping the negative self-talk in its tracks is essential to gaining access to the life you wish to have.

Neuroplasticity allows us to create the pathway which we choose. During meditation, we can truly reprogram our approach to the integration planning step by telling our brain exactly who we are and what we want. If we tell ourselves that we are intelligent due to our thirst for knowledge and methodical preparation, you find yourself becoming that person who prepares in a manner that leads to, you guessed it… intelligence.

A word on nutrition — We will delve much further into nutrition and the various things that we can do to place our bodies in the right mode for exceptional living through a healthy lifestyle. It is worth mentioning here, that mindfulness can be destroyed with bad eating habits or unproven regimens that rob the brain of the necessary nutrients that it needs to perform. Specifically, very low-fat diets are bad for the brain and more importantly for deep mindful thought. The brain uses more energy than any other organ in the human body. Since the brain and the thoughts that it provokes are fueled by what we eat, depriving the brain of the precious nutrients that it needs to produce synaptic responses will also restrict your ability to be aware and conscious. These are both precursors of mindfulness and would obviously impact our abilities to perform exceptionally. Oddly, while the muscles prefer to burn glycogen for energy, the brain prefers to burn healthy fats, restrict these healthy fats from your meal planning and you will get the dreaded brain fog that many low fat dieters speak of. Pay special attention to your meal planning and make sure you are providing the correct amount of macro and micronutrients to the body. The next chapter will shed a great deal of light on this topic.

Continual improvement — We have to improve in order to move forward. Constant practice and conscious thought provoking execution of the 7 steps to mindfulness must become a part of your routine. It can integrate with other things that I have already asked you to do, such as meditation. In order to improve we must measure. Measure the success of the 7 steps by journaling how things are coming along. How many new relationships did you create, and then how many new concepts or thoughtful conversations did that relationship provide.

When we speak of continual improvement in operations or in management systems, we have a four step process: Plan, Execute, Evaluate, and Improve. This should be your goal with self-improvement! In the Enhanced Life Program we plan the improvement, execute the improvement, evaluate what worked and what didn't, and then begin to improve to make it better.

CHAPTER 5

The Body

"Don't you know that you yourselves are God's temple and that
God's Spirit lives in you? If anyone destroys God's temple, God will
destroy him; for God's temple is sacred, and you are that temple."
—1 Corinthians 3:16-17 (NIV)

SO I COULDN'T think of a better quote to start this chapter with. We are indeed 'God's Temple' and those who do not treat it that way, will never gain the insight and experience of the heightened awareness of their supernatural abilities. 'God's Spirit lives in you,' was a cry out to the people of Corinth by the Apostle Paul. He wanted them to understand that the people of the church in Corinth had lost their way, and their connection with the Holy Spirit. This is not unlike where we stand today as a society. It seems appropriate that I write this chapter to you as plea instead of a proposition. We have lost our way and all that we wish to obtain is within our grasp, but we have forgotten that our bodies must first be honed to become a finely tuned instrument of manifestation. In other words, the things that we wish to have in our life are already within our grasp, but we have not trained our three core components to recognize them in a manner that allows them to become reality. While the spirit and the mind must be in unison in order to say yes to this manifestation, the body which is the vessel in which the spirit and the mind must reside, hasn't the power to manifest these gifts alone, though the body can resist them without help from the other core components. In essence, the body can't say yes by itself, but it can say no!

Why is this the case? Our body is and always has been a finely tuned instrument of manifestation. Its ability to nourish the brain which provides the energy source for mindfulness is unmistakable, and nourishing the body with highly processed foods that consume more energy to filter than it provides, will leave you with nothing left for the other faculties of the body that are necessary in order to manifest the things that we wish to achieve in our lives. A perfect analogy is that we are asking our body's to hammer a six inch nail into a thick piece of wood, but we have handed it a plastic spatula to get the job done. Obviously, this won't work and the enlightened state we wish to obtain will never occur.

So how do we treat the body as a temple and maintain our ability to allow the core components to work in unison? Well, the answer is simple, but all too often carrying out the necesarry tasks takes far more discipline than many have and due to this failure, some will convince themselves that it is unimportant. There are 3 steps that we must continue without fail in every stage of our life. Fail to do these 3 tasks and we are in a less than optimal position to become the individual that we so desperately want to be.

Remember when I promised you a practical approach to tapping into a new way of living your life? These 3 steps are as practical as it gets, and although many of the things that we have talked about in previous chapters require the ability to do things that you have likely never tried before, these 3 steps are more about having the desire and discipline to do it.

1. Nourish the body

2. Rest the Body

3. Test the body

If we do all three of these things, we will be prepared to manifest that which we choose, and perfectly align the 3 core components of our existence and allow that connection with the Holy Spirit that you only thought possible in biblical times. Why does it seem that the stories dating back to the times of and even before Christ, seem to describe a people that were much closer with God than we are today? Can't we have that community with God? It doesn't seem as though it can happen to us, or happen to anyone today! Why not you? Why not now? Or, are these 3 steps just too much to ask? This core component was never an issue in the not so distant past, because there were no highly processed foods and prepackaged meals on every corner. We ate what the land provided, and the connection with the universe was almost incidental, or at least wasn't being encumbered by convenience foods and highly processed sugars and fats.

Nourish the Body

Of all of the topics that I will write about in this book, this part I know the most about. My interest in nutrition started a life time ago at the young age of 13. I was one of those kids whose poor eating habits led to poor health and obesity. At a time when acceptance from your peers and relationship building matter the most, I suffered from childhood obesity and was picked on and bullied most of the time. I struggled to play the sports that I loved, and over one summer I lost nearly 55 pounds in 3 months on a starvation diet that left me sick and extremely malnourished. Needless to say, things were not great for me at that stage of my life. While I won't go into the brutality that bullying can create for an adolescent, I will say that even though it was an extremely negative experience for me, it did create some fire from within that made me realize that my body was not in alignment with my mind and spirit, and that the misalignment was causing me significant pain. At thirteen years old, I had no knowledge of nutrition or exercise other than the conditioning that we did in baseball, but after nearly putting myself in the hospital from a diet that consisted of an occasional bite of lettuce or a cucumber, I realized that I needed to know more about nutrition, and from there, my journey of understanding the body began.

Little did I know that it would be the start of an expedition that has led me to the Enhanced Life Performance Program. A journey that started simply with the desire to be as physically fit as I could make my body, turned into a desire to squeeze every inch of productivity out of my being in order to execute at the highest level possible. This desire quickly became a passion, and books like *7 Habits of Highly Effective People,* by Steven Covey, and *The Power of Full Engagement,* by Jim Loehr and Tony Schwartz, fueled my curiosity and led me down the path that I now know as a heightened sense of consciousness and enlightenment. It is quite possible that this enlightenment may have only been meant for me, and was a very personal message. I have often wondered if this book would resonate with anyone else, but as I wrote and shared with close friends whom I hold in high regard, I was asked to continue to share. That really is how this text and the Enhanced Life Performance Program came into being, and has become the standard for many to use to increase their own capacity to tap into the strength of a power that very few people believe even exists, even though we have signs of it every day. It is important to me that you know that this journey started right here, with nutrition.

Let's dive into that nutrition. So the pain of life started me down a path and fueled me to learn, but pain and negativity is not what allowed me to find this supernatural source of energy, it was the positive side of the world that got me there. It is so rewarding when evil and negativity can influence a person to go find the positive and good in our universe, and this is how it happened for me. I tell you this just as a reminder that it truly doesn't matter where you are on your journey, as long as you begin today to remove the negative influences, and humbly seek out the positive forces of our universe and all it has to offer.

Macro nutrients

So how do we prepare the body to be in the best condition for a positive outcome? Let's start with Macro nutrients—macro nutrients consist of the proteins, carbohydrates and fats that we consume in the foods we eat every day. There is much debate waged among the fitness gurus, of the proper amounts that need to be consumed in order to perform optimally at various tasks or sporting goals. Rarely has anyone discussed what those nutrients must be to provide the proper fuel that will predispose the body for integration with the mind and spirit. We bombard our internal systems with highly processed foods laden with pesticides and chemicals and wonder why disease and lack of connection with our universe exists. It is almost as if we have become immune to the idea that additives could possibly be the cause of issues with the health of our core components. I have often said that in order to tap into the supernatural fuel, we must drive in a car that is full of the natural fuel that has been provided by the supernatural. With this in mind, the more organic we become with our fuel source, the higher the quality of our bodily energy becomes. I try to use microwave ovens as little as possible, but I admit sometimes it is difficult to avoid. Many of the properties of organic foods are damaged or altered when utilizing heat, especially intense heat that works at the molecular level. So, before we get to the macro nutrient breakdown, the simple tip I can give you to start this section is this.

Eat as raw and organically as you can. Establish your own garden or make regular trips to your farmers market to obtain organic plant-based foods. Use as little heat as possible, and when using heat, default to a natural source like steam or fire. Lastly, when preparing meals, season with natural sources so that the quest for taste keeps your whole foods, well… whole! Sodium is necessary for life, so be smart with it. Removal of all sodium from your diet would not be healthy, but it has been demonized because we use it today in such copious amounts that the body is often times bombarded with it. Last tip before we get into the details of nourishment is on the topic of hunger. Eat when you are hungry, not when your weak psyche thinks you should eat. Our bodies do a great job of informing us when we need to eat, and typically how much, but generally we eat for reasons other than hunger. Sometimes our body is sending a thirst signal and we interpret it as a hunger request. Make sure we are very in tune with what our body is asking for, and give it the natural sources of the request as often as possible. The summary of these three tips seems so simple that I shouldn't even mention them, but most would improve their bodily nourishment if they just learned to follow these three things:

1. Eat raw organic foods

2. Cook with natural sources of heat and as little of it as possible

3. Learn the messages your body is sending and eat only when hungry

Fats

I started with Fats because of the three macronutrients; fats seem to be the most misunderstood. We have demonized fats over the past 60 years, and it was the government's food pyramid and what I will call conventional wisdom that started it. The problem is that most of this 'conventional wisdom' was just wrong. Let's start by saying this, fat is an awesome energy source and if we train our bodies to use it efficiently, we will not only have a superb energy source that will not lead to additional stored body fat, but we will be feeding our brain with the macronutrient it loves to use for energy. The brain prefers to burn fat as fuel and those who have a very low to no fat diet will complain of issues with memory loss, irritability, loss of focus and a general feeling of mental lethargy. Most western diets are high carbo-hydrate diets with low amounts of the 'good' fats and high amounts of the 'bad fats.' Isn't fat stored in the body as fat, which is bad? The answer here is yes and no, and in the western diet most adipose tissue comes from too many carbohydrates. More to come on the subject of carbohydrates later. Don't get me wrong, adding the wrong fats to your diet is just as problematic, but adding the fats that come from avocados, nut butters, or any other source of a medium chain triglyceride, will actually lead to a more satiated feeling and a more energetic you.

So what fats should I avoid? In a recent article in *WebMD*, Kathleen W. Zelman does a great job of summarizing what types of fats we should add to our diet and which we should remove.

Let's start with the good guys—the unsaturated fats. Unsaturated fats include polyunsaturated fatty acids and monounsaturated fats. Both mono and polyunsaturated fats, when eaten in moderation and used to replace saturated or trans-fats, can help lower cholesterol levels and reduce your risk of heart disease.

Polyunsaturated fats, found mostly in vegetable oils, help lower both blood cholesterol levels and triglyceride levels—especially when you substitute them for saturated fats. One type of polyunsaturated fat is omega-3 fatty acids, whose potential heart-health benefits have gotten a lot of attention. Omega-3s are found in fatty fish (salmon, trout, catfish, mackerel), as well as flaxseed and walnuts. And it is fish that contains the most effective, 'long-chain' type of omega-3s. The American Heart Association recommends eating 2 servings of fatty fish each week.

"Plant sources are a good substitute for saturated or trans-fats, but they are not as effective as fatty fish in decreasing cardiovascular disease," notes A.H. Lichtenstein. Do keep in mind that your twice-weekly fish should not be deep-fat fried!

The other 'good guy' unsaturated fats are monounsaturated fats, thought to reduce the risk of heart disease. Mediterranean countries consume lots of these—primarily in the form of olive oil—and this dietary component is credited with the low levels of heart disease in those countries. Monounsaturated fats are typically liquid at room temperature, but solidify if refrigerated. These heart-healthy fats are typically a good source of the antioxidant vitamin E, a nutrient often lacking in American diets. They can be found in olives, avocados, hazelnuts, almonds, Brazil nuts, cashews sesame seeds, pumpkin seeds, and olive, canola, and peanut oils. Now does this sound like the fat we have been taught is so horrible for us? When the high carbohydrate, low fat diet craze hit the western world; people actually got fatter and sicker as all fats were removed from processed foods and consequently from the western diet. If you remove the fat, you have to replace it with something, and that something back then and now is sugar. So what is the issue with fat and why has it become the red-headed step-child of the macro bunch? Well, ignorance is one and the other is it just has a terrible name. If getting 'fat' is bad, eating 'fat' must be bad as well.

The 'Bad' Fats in Your Diet—Now on to the bad guys. There are two types of fat that should be eaten sparingly: saturated and trans-fatty acids. Both can raise cholesterol levels, clog arteries, and increase the risk for heart disease. Saturated fats are found in animal products (meat, poultry skin, high-fat dairy, and eggs) and in vegetable fats that are liquid at room temperature. We're also hearing a lot these days about trans-fatty acids, or trans fats. There are two types of trans fats: the naturally occurring type, found in small amounts in dairy and meat; and the artificial kind that occur when liquid oils are hardened into 'partially hydrogenated' fats.

Natural trans-fat is not the type that is of concern, especially if you choose low-fat dairy products and lean meats. The real worry in the American diet is the artificial trans-fats. They're used extensively in frying, baked goods, cookies, icings, crackers, packaged snack foods, microwave popcorn, and some margarine. Some experts think these fats are even more dangerous than saturated fats. "Trans-fats are worse than any other fat, including butter or lard," says Michael Jacobson, of the Center for Science in the Public Interest, a nonprofit advocacy group. Research has shown that even small amounts of artificial trans-fats can increase the risk for heart disease by increasing LDL 'bad' cholesterol and decreasing HDL 'good' cholesterol. The American Heart Association (AHA) recommends limiting trans-fat to less than 2 grams per day, including the naturally occurring trans-fats. The U.S. Dietary Guidelines simply recommend keeping consumption of trans-fats as low as possible.

What is the deal with coconut oil, isn't it a saturated fat? Why am I hearing that it's good for me? Coconut oil is a saturated fat, but it is a medium chain triglyceride and yes—92% of the fat in coconut oil is saturated, but what most people are unaware of is that there are different *types* of saturated fats. Some are long-chain (they have 12 or more carbon atoms), and some are medium-chain (fewer than 12 carbon atoms). These various saturated fats do not have the same impact on LDL which is the bad cholesterol. Another long-chain saturated fat, stearic acid, has little impact on LDL cholesterol. Stearic acid is the most common saturated fat in chocolate, which is why chocolate or cocoa butter raises LDL only about one-quarter as much as butter, even though both are about 60% saturated fat.

But coconut and other long-chain saturated fatty acids, like the ones that make up most of the saturated fat in coconut, palm kernel, and palm oils (known as tropical oils), do in fact *raise LDL cholesterol*. These saturated fats are called palmitic, myristic, and lauric acids. They also make up most of the saturated fatty acids in meat, poultry, and dairy fats like milk, butter, and cheese. So, coconut oil has some long chain triglycerides and actually could be negative, and can raise HDL, and a percentage of coconut oil is a medium chain triglyceride so it will lower HDL, hence the confusion.

Other saturated fats that have little impact on LDL cholesterol levels include medium-chain varieties like caproic, caprylic, and capric acids. A small percentage of the saturated fat in coconut oil, about 10%, is made up of these less harmful saturated fatty acids, but virtually all the rest of coconut oil's saturated fat is made up of the long-chain varieties that send LDL soaring so this should be consumed sparingly, but is a good replacement for lard, which has no good properties whatsoever.

The conclusion is that utilization of MCT oil for cooking or use as a dressing is actually good for your LDL, and those fats can be used for energy, especially if you are typically a lower carbohydrate eater. This energy is predominately used by the brain, and in our last chapter we discussed how important the brain is in the pursuit of mindfulness. Coconut oil is not 'bad' for you but it isn't the healthy equivalent to fat either. 90% of the fat is a long chain fatty acid. Here is a great chart of fats and what type they are:

Saturated Fats or trans fatty acids	Polyunsaturated Fats	Monounsaturated Fats
Butter	Corn oil	Canola oil
Lard	Fish oils	Almond oil
Meat, lunchmeat	Soybean oil	Walnut oil
Poultry, poultry skin	Safflower oil	Olive oil
Coconut products	Sesame oil	Peanut oil
Palm oil, palm kernel oil and products	Cottonseed oil	Avocado
Dairy foods (other than skim)	Sunflower oil	Olives
Partially hydrogenated oils	Nuts and seeds	Peanut butter

Carbohydrates

It seems like lately the pendulum has moved to meal plans very restrictive of carbohydrates, and for the most part many should consider this. If you consume carbohydrates, as most do in the western world, you are probably consuming an inordinate amount and this is likely causing many other issues within in your life. Carbohydrates are likely the reason why so many of us have heart disease and diabetes and many other weight related ailments like hypertension, anxiety and depression. If there was one macro that I felt was the cause for people losing touch with who they really are and who they could become, carbohydrates would be it. Now, even though there are times throughout the year when I reduce my carbohydrate intake to much lower than normal levels, this doesn't mean that *you* should remove carbs from your diet. Carbohydrates—when consumed with a purpose—can bring massive amounts of energy and much needed muscle glycogen to your body. Here is the simple truth about carbohydrates.

The body catabolizes all carbohydrates into glucose, and once in the blood stream only three things can happen. It can be used immediately for energy, stored in the muscle as glycogen, or, the remaining amounts unused by the body will be transformed into fatty acids, which can later be stored as body fat. For elite athletes this rarely happens due to the dietary needs that accompany the intense training they go through. With all the talk about carbohydrates making us fat, we have lost sight of the fact that this only occurs if we don't use the carbohydrates that we eat for fuel. Carbohydrates are an essential part of our diet, but type and timing of when you eat them is pretty important to athletes, especially those who are putting serious demands on their bodies. Since most of us are not elite athletes, this is where the over-consumption tends to rear its ugly head. Here is the issue. Are you an elite athlete? Our western culture consumes massive amounts of carbohydrates assuming that 'low fat' is a good thing. Anytime we reduce our fat content in our meal plan, we typically replace those calories with carbohydrates.

Carbohydrates—in the form of bread, rice, cereal, pasta, and other grains—could be a part of your daily food consumption, but carbohydrates found in other foods, including vegetables, legumes, nuts, and soy should be the carbohydrates that are first on our list. Low carbohydrate diets are becoming popular, even among elite athletes, but like any good thing, some people, without good dietary information, tend to choose plans that make them 'look' good as opposed to 'feel good' or perform at a high level.

The latest diet craze called Keto dieting, which is where almost all carbohydrate sources are eliminated from the diet, forces the body to utilize ketones as the main energy source. This diet has been surrounded by much controversy. Does it work? Well, studies show that it does if the goal is fat loss. Typically, we have an unlimited store of fat for energy because the body will convert all excess calories over our TDEE (Total Daily Energy Expenditure) as fat. I would caution you, however, that this type of diet is not for everyone. If you currently eat like the normal western person, you will go through carbohydrate withdrawals and for 4 or 5 days feel like you have the flu. This is known as the 'keto flu.' This feeling does go away as your body converts to burning fat as its main energy source, but how you tolerate this is specific to your daily activities and is specific to you and your metabolism.

Keep in mind that glycogen stored in the liver provides energy for vital functions like brain activity, red blood cell production, and kidney cell regeneration. The glycogen stores that are in the muscles cannot be used for those vital functions. The brain prefers to burn fat as energy and often does, especially when we are in a fasted state. So while some sports performance could suffer from low carbohydrate diets that place you in glycogen debt, other strength related sports have shown improvement when limiting the number of carbohydrates you consume.

We have talked a great deal about the need for the brain to be in top working order to achieve mindfulness. Removing fat from our diets and replacing it with a simple carbohydrate is the last thing we want to do. The brain needs these essential fats. That doesn't mean we need to remove carbohydrates altogether, nor does it mean we need to go back to the days of unbridled carbohydrate loading. Spikes in blood sugar will drastically reduce your ability to concentrate, but so will low blood sugar levels. In response to a spike in glucose, your pancreas pumps out insulin to transport it to cells throughout your body. This process causes your blood sugar and insulin levels to move up and down rapidly, often leaving you feeling fatigued and hungry.

So, what do we do? The answer is not as simple as you might think. The amount and type of carbohydrates is specific to every person, and is dependent on the type of exercise that is being executed. What we are ultimately trying to accomplish is to store just enough glycogen to support vital functions as well as fuel your daily lives at work and at play, but not an ounce more. This, to a certain degree is trial and error, and will take time to develop the best mix of complex and simple carbohydrates within your nutrition plan.

Typically, when we talk about nutrition, the conversation always moves to weight loss because most people need to lose a few. Weight Loss or more appropriately described, 'fat loss,' has to be addressed separately than fueling and enhanced performance. Don't get me wrong, one can lead to the other, but it is better to remove unwanted fat that hinders enhanced performance and then work to maintain that state of equilibrium between fat loss and gain. Excess amounts of fat cry out for more carbohydrate foods to help maintain the current fat levels. These signals impact your hormones and your desire for certain foods. This can be a major distraction while trying to find the connection between your mindfulness behaviors and the body that carries it out.

Common sense and a closely kept food diary goes a long way, but in order to think clearly and precisely, jump higher and run faster than you ever have, and execute at an extremely high level at both work and at play, your body has to be working optimally. To do that, the type and amount of carbohydrates you consume must be precise.

If this is not something you feel you can accomplish on your own, contacting one of our life coaches or a personal trainer that you trust at your gym may be an answer. Short of that, an over simplification of this could be of great help, depending on your goals and current body composition, but as a general rule overgeneralization never seems to work. First and foremost before changing your eating habits seek out professional advice from a doctor. Sadly most doctors know less about this than they should and oddly nutritionists know even less. Take special care of choosing a person who has a track record and has done extensive research in this area..

Even though I should refrain from generalizing, I do want to help

ENHANCED LIFE PERFORMANCE

if I can. If you are trying to reduce your fat stores, and utilize that fat as fuel for the brain and body, start by consuming 15 to 25% of your daily calories as carbohydrates. If you are looking to maintain your weight, you might be better served at 30%. If you are an athlete that endurance trains, you need to increase this amount based on the demand you are placing on your body during training, but if your body can burn fat readily for fuel – this state is called "fat-adapted" then keep carbohydrates low and the fat fuel source and ketones will drive you through your training. Remember, if you are using carbohydrates as the energy source, these carbohydrates MUST be slow burning. Note: this is NOT scientifically precise, and you need to consider many other things before making this your nutrition plan, but as a rule of thumb this can help you get through this phase and into a much better state of mind. I could write an entire book on nutrition, and one day I may. The chapter on carbohydrates would be the focus of the book, because it is truly the macronutrient that hinders or helps our performance the most. Fats and proteins support all the necessary functions for us to achieve at a high level, but carbohydrates, in my opinion, are the only macronutrient that can not only say yes to an enhanced self, they can also say no by clouding our bodies with the wrong hormones at the wrong time. Remember stay with slow burning carbohydrates like brown rice, sweet potatoes, and leafy and cruciferous vegetables.

Protein

Protein's main responsibility is to help in tissue repair. Protein, once digested in the body, breaks down into amino acids. These amino acids are transported to the various areas of the body for repair. Having adequate sources of protein is essential for your body and is required to create structure and function of body tissues. These tissues include body organs, hair and skin. Proteins are also used in membranes, such as glycoproteins. When broken down into amino acids, they are used as precursors to nucleic acid, co-enzymes, hormones, immune response, cellular repair, and other molecules essential for life.

So, it appears obvious that protein is an important macronutrient for our quest of achieving the most optimal self, but how much should we have? This topic is controversial because there has been some link to certain cancers based on overconsumption of protein. It is hard to say if this is specific to protein only, because there are so many things that protein impacts. We have extensively discussed the difference between the needs of elite athletes and those of moderately active individuals that are likely reading this book. You will have to be the judge of what area you fall into. If you are vigorously exercising for more than two hours per day, you are beginning to approach elite athletic status. The rule of thumb for protein is a bit less controversial than that of carbohydrates and fats. While I never prefer broad generalizations for macronutrient recommendations, I feel more comfortable making suggestions about quantity of protein than any other macro.

Why is this? Quite simply we know more about protein and how it impacts the body than any of the other two macronutrients. This allows us to be a bit more general in our approach. I will break this into four categories to try and be at least directionally more precise. If you were enrolled in one of our programs, this would be much more precise than what I am about to suggest, but nonetheless, this will give you an idea of the direction you should be heading.

- Sedentary Males — .7 grams of protein per pound of body weight
- Sedentary Females —.6 grams of protein per pound of body weight
- Active Males — 1 gram of protein per pound of body weight
- Active Females — .8 grams of protein per pound of body weight

It is my opinion that proteins should never go above 1 gram per pound of body weight, unless you are in the category of elite athlete and those protein calories are going to good use.

Please remember that brain cells communicate with one another via chemical messengers called neurotransmitters (we discussed neuroplasticity already), which are usually made of amino acids, the building blocks of protein. A healthy brain produces hundreds of neurotransmitters needed for regular maintenance of the brain and needs proteins to do so. Make sure that this is a regular part of your meal plan. If you are a vegetarian, this can be challenging and you may need to supplement with various plant based protein powders in order to reach these numbers.

If you wish to execute at a high level, proteins must be a priority. If I find myself in a rare situation where the only thing I can eat is a fast food meal, I would grab a burger and throw everything but the meat away. I can skip some carbs, and I can skip some fats, albeit not often, but protein is essential!

Rest the Body

If there is any one thing I struggle with the most on the physical side of things, rest would be at the top of the list. I struggle with this because I enjoy physical activity so much, and I find rest and relaxation boring and a bit lazy. Rest sometimes for me must be forced. I actually have to schedule sleep at times, because I just plain don't do it. I love to get up early in the morning and write, enjoying this time when the house is quiet and everyone else is asleep. It is 4 A.M. as I am typing this, but I know at some point I will have to rest my body to prepare myself for the next exceptional day. The importance of rest is a well-studied and often discussed topic, but we don't think about how rest can reconnect the body, mind and spirit with one another as it goes through repair during the sleep cycle. Not just for the body, but also for the mind. That being said, everybody is different. I can get by on 7 hours of sleep per night and never feel fatigued. Anything less, at some point in the week, I have to play catch up. Nothing that a restful afternoon nap could not cure, but if I go too long without scheduling such an event, my exceptional self begins to dull in its ability to execute. When I realize this is happening, I do everything in my power at that very moment to schedule the soonest rest period that I can find.

Along with recovery, we engage in tissue repair and the secretion of growth hormone during sleep. There are many studies that shows the brain activity during sleep is off the charts and can actually help you problem solve during the day. This gives literal meaning to the old saying, 'Let me sleep on it.'

Typically, we are told that 8 hours of sleep per night is optimal, but this is a very personal number. I track my resting heart rate and I notice that lack of recovery makes my resting heart rate increase. This obviously can impact my health and is a good indicator that I could be overtraining by not allowing my body enough time to recover. The best way to combat that is to curl up in bed and get a long and restful night's sleep. If you struggle to get to sleep naturally, you should try 100-200 milligrams of magnesium and 5mg of melatonin, this can help you relax and get to sleep, but as always check with your physician before taking any supplements for any reason.

Test the Body

Now we're talking! Let's test the body. If you are uncomfortable, you are heading in the right direction. We must test the body in order to push it past the limits that you have set for it. It is truly surprising how far the body can go.

Going back to the book, *The Power of Full Engagement,* rest was not the only thing that they cited as important. Elite athletes train in very specific ways. Many of them go really hard for a period of time and even push past the limits that they once thought possible. Then they rest. The rest is obviously important, but pushing past what they originally felt that they were capable of creates a new normal, resulting in overall growth in the body's ability to withstand the next test.

I would compare this to the 4 minute mile. On May 6, 1954, Roger Banister broke the 4 minute mile, a feat that no one had ever accomplished. In fact, many argued that a human would never be able to do it. Roger used imagery during his training and often visualized the achievement in order to create a sense of certainty in his mind and body that it could be done. In fact, he convinced himself he had already done it. Even more interesting is that less than one year later, another runner accomplished the same feat. This is a great example of once we push ourselves past what we thought was possible; it becomes the new normal for us. Sometimes even watching someone else do it allows you to think that we can do it as well.

We should do this with our work and try to stretch our ability to consume information and make actionable data from it. I find myself doing this with my writing. I will typically plan a day that I will write even more than makes me comfortable. I push past that point where I just want to stop because my brain is tired, but I dredge on. The key is that after this session, I do get some rest and make sure that my activities later that day are not cognitively or intellectually challenging (this is difficult for me because everything seems to challenge my intellect ….. I parenthetically digress.) Resting the brain and the body should happen often, but only after you have properly tested it.

As a bodybuilder, of which I have a lot of experience, this concept of pushing past failure is a regular occurrence. Whether we are doing drop sets, pyramids, or spot assisted, we are always finding ways to make the muscle group we are training uncomfortable as hell! Then, we rest that body part to allow it to recover—bigger, stronger and better. Then, we do it all over again.

I would argue that you should apply these concepts to your work! Read the book, *The Power of Full Engagement,* and you will not only know why, but also exactly how to do it! In essence, it is just like an elite athlete blasting a muscle, running a mile, or challenging the psychological aspects of the sport. Challenge yourself at work; go hard for an extended period of time with hyper focus and hyper productivity. Then allow yourself time to rest.

Summary and Continual Improvement

The body is an important part of the three core components. It is the vessel that houses the mind and the spirit, and the efficiency of that vessel is crucial to becoming the exceptional supercharged person that you wish to become. Let's summarize our discussion and then move on to other chapters tying this into practical use. You have to constantly evaluate and tweak your body and its responses to the stressors and challenges of life. What works for you at one exercise or stress level, may not in the future. In order to keep your body efficient and in top working order we must do the following things consistently.

Nourish The Body
- Eat Raw Organic Foods
- Cook with natural sources of heat and as little of it as possible
- Learn the messages your body is sending and eat only when hungry
- Balance your macronutrients

Rest the Body
- 8 hours of sleep – this is different for everyone, but good rule of thumb
- Listen to the body for signs of diminished recovery
- Test the Body
- Push past failure
- Push your mental capacities as well
- Rest

References

Journal of the Academy of Nutrition and Dietetics: Position of the Academy of Nutrition and Dietetics: Dietary Fatty Acids for Healthy Adults

NYU Langone Medical Center: Medium-Chain Triglycerides

USDA National Nutrient Database: Vegetable Oil, Palm Kernel

USDA National Nutrient Database: Oil, Coconut

USDA National Nutrient Database: Milk, Whole, 3.25 Percent Milkfat, Without Added Vitamin A and Vitamin D

USDA National Nutrient Database: Milk, Nonfat, Fluid, With Added Vitamin A and Vitamin D (Fat Free or Skim)

USDA National Nutrient Database: Butter, Salted

USDA National Nutrient Database: Cheese, Cheddar

USDA National Nutrient Database: Fast Foods, Biscuit, With Ham

Brandeis University: Schuster Institute for Investigative Journalism: Outline of Production: Palm Fruit to Product

CHAPTER 6

Three Components, One Result

"You don't get results, by focusing on results.
You get results by focusing on the actions that produce results!"
—Mike Hawkins

WE HAVE DISCUSSED at length the 3 core components and how to have a better connection with each. Successfully improving the health of all three of these components will allow you to live a much more fulfilled life and as we get into the details of Life Planning, you will recognize it places you in a state of alignment with what God and the universe He commands wants for you. In essence, not just the planning, but the execution begins to fall into place because you are congruent with what it is you are supposed to be doing. You have created your mission, defined your core purpose and personified your core with clear mental imagery. This will lead to a more fulfilled life and once we are fulfilled, we allow room for charity which enhances your community, which leads to legacy! The progress of these steps is unmistakable, and as I experienced them being checked off the list one-by-one, my life and those around me got to enjoy a person that was very different than whom I had been before.

These three core components combine to create the single result of legacy. But, does this happen automatically? Once we hone the spirit mind and body, do we stop wandering aimlessly just because we are in this enhanced state of being? Well, of course not, and this is where the path becomes extremely practical and we show the steps of how to achieve this supernatural version of self.

If you were a corporate customer of mine and you were asking me to evaluate any project or initiative, the approach would look identical in business as it does in life. It is straight forward and is a normal part of any management or project framework and should be considered for life as well.

- Plan
- Execute
- Evaluate
- Improve

These 4 steps, if we were to use them to road map our lives, would provide us all the information that we need to achieve and execute every day at a very high level.

Legacy is not created without a plan. Think of any famous person in history, they didn't walk aimlessly about their entire lives. Some may have for a time, but it wasn't until they laid out their plan that they began to achieve their legacy.

Why didn't I start with this and skip the hokey meditation, feel-good stuff? Because that hokey meditation, feel-good stuff is the essential first step, before any plan can be made. Regardless of the plan, and despite a flawless execution, if your 'Legacy Plan' is not in congruence with what God and the universe intends, you will never be happy. Let me take this opportunity to make one thing clear. There are some who have the appearance of success and have everything one might imagine would accompany a great legacy plan, but if it is not in congruence with what the universe has in mind, then chances are they are not happy or fulfilled. We have witnessed many people with the world at their feet commit suicide or live a life of utter despair, despite being surrounded by the wealth of the world.

Let's touch on all four of these steps in life planning, and then the next four chapters will be a deep dive into how we execute using practical tools and give examples of how the legacy plan unfolds.

Plan

I call it a 'Legacy Plan' because we all want to leave a legacy behind and leave our mark on the world. You can't do it without planning to do it, and even if only a very small group of people remember you and carry on your life examples—coaching, and teaching—your efforts to garner legacy will be filled with legacy impressions which are incredibly satisfying to us here on earth. Our legacy plan must be as detailed as a map. This map must give us a detailed turn-by-turn instruction set that will help you carry out the activities necessary to achieve legacy. Leave a step out and you are leaving it to chance. Any female that has gone to a sporting event in a new city with their husband or significant other, has had the experience when he says, "I know where I am going!" She knows what he's really thinking but not saying, might well be, 'I have no freaking clue where we are!' The man feels as if he knows because for one it's a sporting event so his testosterone naturally has sudden directional gifts that will help him navigate, and second, men just hate asking for directions... I digress.

I use this analogy because the way a man feels about a trip to a sporting event is the way we all feel about our lives. We feel as if we are predisposed to 'know' where we are going, but we never step back to even see where we are on the map. There are many consequences of this type of action, and typically, it creates a situation that places you in a less than desirable location in life. Even worse, you may be on the right path and have never taken the time to enjoy the fact that you are there because you didn't take the time to know that you arrived. So many people set these grand goals and often times blow through them, but never take the time to humbly thank the universe or the Holy Spirit for providing the means to have it, or even just stop to take a deep breath and say, "Wow we did it!"

When I was in high school we lived in a small 3-bedroom house that at the time was the picture of middle class America. The truth is my dad was gone, and my mom was broke trying to raise two hungry boys. Let's just say that financially speaking, ends were not meeting. I remember clearly visualizing the type of house I wanted to live in. A big, three story house with a basement that had a gym and a cool man cave. Anybody want to venture a guess at what my current house looks like? Right, a big three story house with a basement that holds a gym and man cave. Ask me if I took the time to congratulate my family and give thanks for it. At that time, I didn't. I just woke up and went back to the grindstone to get the next 'thing.' Today, with my new knowledge of what the universe provides, I see it differently. Today, I thank the Holy Spirit each day, and not necessarily for the physical house that we love and live in, I humbly thank Him for the abilities he gave me to afford them and the knowledge that my house is only a home if my family feels safe and secure in it. My house is a place of solace and rest, it invites you to stay and really live and be a part of our small family community.

I share this with you because I don't want you to make the same mistake. Be specific about what you want, and be careful, because the more detailed it is, the better the chances of it showing up in your life. Is this some hocus-pocus magic that makes things appear? No, it is the clear unobstructed view of what you are trying to accomplish, and when you give the 3 components of your being that clarity, what you can achieve becomes far easier than when you are blindly throwing darts at a target.

So, what are the steps of building the Legacy Plan? We will discuss this in great detail in the next chapter.

Execute

I have said before that I place a very high value on execution. One of the first things that I evaluate when I engage in executive coaching is to look at what the executive 'executes' on a daily basis. What is his or her 'functional' role within the company? Regardless if they are a Vice President or the CEO, if they do not execute at a high level, existing within the organization on a strategic level only, I find that the organization rarely has respect for this person. Consequently they typically are not very effective. You must 'do' something and be deliberate about it.

Our Legacy Plan is no different. The Legacy Plan will be difficult to write, mainly because we rarely look at our lives in this much detail. If we are successful at writing the legacy plan in a fashion that truly makes it actionable, then the only thing left to do is to begin! When do we start? We start now! Why wait? It is your life, and trust me, most people die knowing only that legacy does not come easy. Executing at a high level is driven by the mind and the body, oftentimes more than your spirit. Remember, the spirit has limitless universal power and energy. Your body and mind, however, depend on your discipline to provide it power and energy. What we eat, drink and expose our bodies and minds to plays a crucial role in how we execute.

Let me give you an example. I once managed a gentleman who was a little overweight and had no plans to change this about himself. He enjoyed food and the comfort it gave him. Naturally, he was a low-key guy and his speech patterns were very monotone. His leadership abilities were challenged by the fact that his people did not see him as a dynamic personality, and because of his speech patterns and monotone approach, his meetings were real snoozers! I noticed that most of his important meetings were after lunch, and inevitably, his lunches consisted of high carbohydrate, high fat meals that left him even more sedentary and 'low key.' No wonder his team was not inspired, he was in a fog of sugar and insulin, and his body was screaming, "It's NAP time!" instead of, "It's GO time!" I digress. Had he moved his meeting to the morning, he would have had an improvement in his ability to be more dynamic, just because his body and mind were more alert. The right thing to do would have been to hone his body and mind to an instrument that was prepared to be an executive in this high paced successful business, but he chose a different route. Eventually, this person moved on, because his team was no longer behind him and he couldn't adjust quickly enough to regain the respect he once had. Please understand, I am not saying that people who carry a few extra pounds can't execute at a high level. I am saying that people who are unhealthy or unhappy, generally cannot execute at the level they generally would if their health or disposition was in a better place.

Execution, therefore, is not just about doing things or checking something off the list, it is doing it with your 3 core components acting as one, and doing it with the thought of leaving a legacy. My epitaph states, "I will stand before God knowing I had done all I can!" This holds true at work, and for my family and my friends. So, when I execute, I freaking bring it!

Evaluate

Evaluation, along with thoughtful contemplation is key to the Enhanced Life Program. The steps that we go through during evaluation allow us to verify whether we truly are following the plan and executing at the highest level possible. The evaluation step is a step of measurement and a guide for improvement. As we create the Legacy Plan, there must be milestone stops along the way that allow us to measure if the path that we are on is indeed tracking to the result and/or goal. Legacy Impressions allow us to verify that we are on track for the final goal of leaving behind a legacy, but these measurement steps are far more specific and practical. Leaving a legacy is an outcome that will be achieved if we follow the process. The process is created with the plan, and the important points of the plan must have a measurement component or how would you know if you were tracking toward the goal? For example, if one of the steps in your plan was to have your house paid off in seven and a half years as opposed to the 15 year mortgage, you could easily track the various milestone points as you endeavored to pay the house off early. If you are 3 years in, and have only paid off 1 percent of the mortgage then you know you are behind. This simple example is just one of many measurement components that you need to have in your Legacy Plan, and you should execute at a minimum, a quarterly review of your plan along with the results of the milestone measurements to see how you are tracking. This will give you an overview of what you need to focus on in the next quarter, and allow you the opportunity to make small changes along the way that will impact the outcome. The other value of the evaluation step is to restate the 'Why' of the Legacy Plan and verify that it is congruent with what the universe wants you to be doing. Using the same example, if the mortgage is on track at the halfway point, but you hate your job and everything about it, you are not in alignment. Most people would ignore this and not realize that the negative feelings about the job may be impacting everything else. So, great, the house is paid off early, but your spirit has been sacrificed for a monetary goal that is impeding your ability to have fulfilment and eventually give back. The least thing that you must do in your evaluation phase, in your quarterly review, is check your Legacy Impressions. If you have gone through 2 quarterly reviews with no Legacy Impressions, you are not on the right track and your Legacy Plan needs attention.

Improve

So far, at the end of each chapter on spirit, mind and body, we provided an approach to continual improvement. The Continual Improvement step is the cornerstone of the Enhanced Life Performance Program. It is the extra one degree further that allows us to step back and look at the entire body of work and make small changes that will allow improvement in the next iteration. Many people, both in their personal and professional careers, spend an inordinate amount of time in the planning phase and never get to the execution phase, because they are seeking perfection. Perfection is not only impossible, but it is not necessary and we must understand that positive activity begets more positive activity. So just start, and start now! The evaluation and improvement phases will allow you the opportunity to make changes to the plan or to the way you are executing the plan. This will make the next time that step is executed much more fulfilling, and potentially rewarding both to the quality of your life and the progression toward creating a legacy impression. We have all heard of the KISS method. Keeping the improvement simple is a key to tracking its effectiveness. Small changes are what is in order here, not multiple or drastic swings. If we do this in the improvement phase it is far more difficult to track effectiveness. If you find sweeping changes are needed, it might be time to reevaluate the planning phase to see what might have gone wrong.

Now that we have introduced the next practical phase of the Enhanced Life Program, I wanted to remind you that these four steps are much more impactful if you are in a good place with your spirit, mind, and body connection. Don't expect that connection to be perfect, however. Your connection with the universe and the power that it can give you will always vacillate between a moderate connection and some days, a very strong connection. I will tell you it is better to get started and make small changes than to await the perfect connection to your core components, because we should always seek improvement to that connection and feel a bit like we are not 'perfect' in that approach.

The next four chapters will break down each step and this practical approach is exactly what you need to achieve the exceptional life that you wish to lead. Don't assume you know how or what to do with the next four steps, because even if you do, the chances that you are actually doing them is slim. If you were carrying out these steps and doing it to a level in which it had become habit, you likely wouldn't be reading this book, you would be writing it.

CHAPTER 7

The Legacy Plan

"A goal without a Plan is just a wish."
Antoine de Saint-Exupery

OUR APPROACH TO planning life is centered on the idea that extraordinary people need to lead extraordinary lives, so that they may impact others to build and leave a legacy. The Legacy Plan, as it is aptly named, focuses on the six areas of fulfillment that assist you in leaving a legacy. We are wired to give back to the universe that supports us. We are also wired for success, and success is in abundance for everyone who wants it. There is no need to assume that there is a finite amount of success. Money, happiness, and fulfillment are all in play, and do not assume that there is a limited amount that we are all trying to get a piece of. First of all, we will never be in a state where all people will aspire to have extraordinary lives, but what we have to come to realize is the universe was designed that way. The issue is, especially today, the human condition will not allow it. Remember that pesky little concept of free will? All humans have free will to choose, and while having an extraordinary life is truly attainable, the simple truth is in today's society, it is far easier not to. Some of you are so wired for success that you didn't realize this to be. Some think the competition is far too great, and that the limited resources of the universe had passed you by. The fact is, the universe was designed

111

to provide for all, we as humans chose to assume that it was limited. Regardless, you are planning YOUR life and not the lives of others. A major part of that plan is integration into the lives of those you care for and wish to impact positively. We have come to learn this is more for you than it is for them, for humility and charity are repaid tenfold! You should bank legacy impressions as if they were cold hard cash, because success begets success, and the universe rewards those who help others. The world and the society that inhabits it, rewards those who have success, typically with... you guessed it, money. Now, money is not the goal, nor is it a sin. Money is a unit of measure, it is not measuring your value or worth, money is a unit of measure of your ability to consume. That's it! It means nothing! Have you ever noticed that we tend to receive things when we STOP obsessing over them? Money is exactly that way. Focus on the process of leaving a legacy, impacting others, becoming a role model that your kids, family and friends are proud of, and two things happen. You won't care as much about your ability to consume worldly goods, and ironically, your ability to do so will exponentially increase. Add to that, acts of charity and the universe sees you as someone that can handle the very success that you so desperately want.

We have been through the exercises of the epitaph and the t-shirt slogan. These will be very helpful in your Legacy Plan. Remember that while planning your Legacy, having your significant other on board is necessary, they have to be just as committed to your plan as you are, because they can't force you to achieve your plan, but they can hinder you from doing so every step of the way. Besides, whoever dies first will need the other to carry out your last requests, and trust me; if you do this right there will be a lot to do after your passing.

Instead of the question, 'What do you want to do with your life?' it is more important to decide, 'Who do you want to be?' It is far too cliché to ask you to do what you love, because if you are like me, you may love many things. I would start with 'Who do I want to be?' and identify what profession supports me to be that person. In other words, priests and members of the clergy are not the only people 'called' to do something. Policeman, teachers, and social workers are all called to do what they do for one reason or another, and often are successful beyond measure.

The steps that we went through in the first few chapters will most definitely help you with this process. Just like our core purpose, we need to dig deeper than we ever have, because our first answers to questions of 'Who do I want to be?' are rarely the answers that create fulfillment in life. Let me give you an example.

I love the step of 'test the body.' I do it daily, and exercise for me has become a way of life. I have coached, been a martial arts instructor and have managed many people in my various careers, and it would be easy for me to say that the 'job' or the 'what I want to do?' is a gym owner or a well-respected sensei. That, however; is not the answer to the question of whom I wish to be. The person and the life I wish to lead is undoubtedly that of teacher or mentor, and there are many traits that God has gifted me with that could allow me to do just that. Incidentally, there are numerous careers that will allow me to achieve this goal. My Legacy Plan is mapped out to allow me to achieve that goal. To clarify, my job is not 'Who I am,' however, 'Who I am,' impacts how I do my job. I have purposely searched for a career path that allows me to mentor, coach and teach, and this is why today, I am the Chief Operations Officer at a regional systems integration company. I get to mentor, coach, and teach, plus utilize my knowledge of Information Technology. But most importantly, I can expand my ability and focus on helping others achieve what they want to achieve. Again 'Who I am' is allowing me to do what I want to do.

Before we go through a step by step process, and in all essence, provide you with the template to help you along the way, let's cover one last topic. No one is responsible for your life and your legacy other than you. You must take extreme ownership of your life and plan it per the legacy you wish to leave and in sync with the spiritual and universal power that you will call upon to help carry out the daily tasks that will get you there. This book in fact, is a step in my own journey to legacy, but my intent of writing it is not to be on the New

York Times Best Seller List, although I admit that I believe it will be... I digress... again.

No, it is not a list or a total number of books or a number of adopters of the ELP philosophy that drives me. This book is being written for two reasons. The first and most important is that I want my kids to have a manual for life, a primer on life preparation. I want all four of my beautiful kids to hand this book to their children and their children's children, and know that this is how 'Pops' lived his life and why he passed over to the next adventure knowing he had done all that he could. See, this is part of my plan to leave a legacy. The second reason is more about my career, which indirectly leads to legacy, but is directly impactful to my legacy plan. I want to use this book and a more condensed version of this book as a workbook in our coaching sessions. I have used these concepts and only recently realized that a better illustration of the process was needed. This allows me an even better opportunity to impact people positively. It is worth mentioning that success in business has always been within my grasp because of my process and work ethic, but it wasn't until I started focusing on helping others that the success I had experienced became fulfilling!

So let's build the legacy plan template and get started on creating a plan that aligns you with your heart, your talents and your legacy.

The Legacy Plan Template

If you have begun to meditate with some success, it might be a good idea to clear your mind and start this process with a 10 to 20-minute meditation which will put you in alignment with the Holy Spirit and the universe that He commands. This will guarantee a meaningful approach to the next steps in the Legacy Plan process.

It is time for you to be the fly on the wall at your own funeral and listen in on what your family and friends are saying about you. You may remember these statements in Chapter 1. This is where you begin to find the common things of what you feel are important to you.

1. *In my lifetime I want to accomplish* _____

_____

2. *In my lifetime I want* _____, _____,

and_____ *to know that I am* _____.

3. *In my lifetime I want my immediate family to know me as*

_____ *and* _____.

4. *In my lifetime I want strangers to know me for*

_____.

5. *If I could give the world one thing back (service to the community, knowledge of some topic, teaching a Sunday school class) as a thank you for all of the great things I have been blessed with and had the discipline to nurture, it would be*

_____.

Create your Core Purpose statement utilizing the common statements that have appeared in the exercise above. I have listed mine and you will see that nowhere in this core purpose does it list what 'job' or 'career' that I wish to choose. It is a deeper look into my soul and the desire to leave a legacy.

Core Purpose (Mission Statement): Through the sweat of my brow, the gift of my mind and the foundations of my faith, I want to be the best father, husband, friend and man that I can be! The world has far too few real men left and I choose to do the difficult task when others choose easy! I choose to stay late when others leave early and I choose to take responsibility when others cower. Knowing that I had done everything in my power on earth to stand before God when my time arrives, I will do so with a clear conscience, fulfilled heart and satisfied mind, but with curiosity of the things to come in paradise! I am a warrior and I am called to conquer and take extreme ownership of my life!

Epitaph: I will stand before God knowing I have done all that I can!

Family's Statement (what my family will say about me): No matter what the situation, Pops was always willing to give of his physical or mental strength, to make us stronger to get through what we once thought was insurmountable.

Stranger Statement (what strangers will say about me): By placing an extremely high value on execution, It is apparent that coaching and teaching is his gift, and he chooses to use it in a manner that makes others believe in themselves even when they believed in nothing.

T-Shirt slogan: Civilize the mind! Make Savage the Body!

As you can see with the examples given above, there is an enormous amount of content that will provide clues dictating what you need to be doing from a tactical perspective to lead a fulfilled and exceptional life. The next step in the process will define the avenue or vehicle needed to achieve the Core Purpose that you have listed. Let's create a list of what we call 'I will' statements that will further detail the goals that will put you in alignment with your core purpose.

I will leave a legacy!

I will be fulfilled!

I will mentor and coach!

I will help people laugh and smile!

I will be a great father, husband and friend!

I will be a trusted advisor!

I will be respected in the community!

I will be in alignment with the Holy Spirit!

I will make my body a precision tool of execution!

I will be a warrior for the weak and less fortunate!

I will take and maintain extreme ownership of my life.

These are my 'I will' statements. Regardless of my career path, there are certain truths about my 'I will' statements that must be considered in order for me to map out my Legacy Plan. Those truths are exposed as we align our spirit, mind and body with what the Holy Spirit has gifted us to perform on behalf of humanity. In other words, I cannot succumb to the simple pleasures of the flesh, if those pleasures do not allow me to maintain my body as a precision instrument of execution. I cannot succumb to my ego if I want to make others laugh or smile. I cannot succumb to lethargy or laziness if I want to mentor or coach. These are simple truths that become very apparent, and since I already know the 'Why' behind the things I do (leaving a legacy), my journey becomes far more gratifying and fulfilling.

Now that you know the 'why' and your core purpose, your epitaph is written, you know exactly what strangers and family members will say after your death, you have your own T-shirt slogan and your 'I will' statements, you are set. You can now begin planning the tactical events of the day, week, month, quarter, year, five-year and long term activities that lead to the legacy you wish to become.

Most planners begin with the end in mind, and in essence we did that in the earlier chapters, we know we want to leave a legacy, we know we want to be fulfilled along the way, but we don't know practically how to achieve all of that just yet because the plan is not in place. It should be as clear as a preflight checklist. Incidentally, the preflight checklist is extremely precise because... lives depend on it. Why then, would we choose to be vague when we know our life depends on the Legacy Plan that we create and tweak today? We will begin with the five-year plan and work our way downward to daily, and then take the five-year plan up to Legacy, so the plan will always pivot on the fifth-year mark. Why do we do this you may wonder? Every major change in life takes time to grow, and if this is the first time you have taken on such a challenge, you will find that you experience great things very early on, but the real magic will exist in the continual improvement that we embrace in our lives as the plan progresses and you do your quarterly 'Legacy Reviews.' So the plan gets better and better with every Legacy Review (a concept we will discuss later), and with each tweak of the details.

CHAPTER **8**

Five-Years Out

WE HAVE 6 areas of fulfillment to consider when planning in order to reach a life of legacy, a life that is worth passing on. These are in order, but not necessarily in order of importance; instead, they are in the order of priority.

- Faith
- Family
- Career
- Financial
- Community
- Charity

Remember, we are tapping into a supernatural power, an exceptional way of living that reaches beyond the ordinary. These 6 areas of fulfillment will feed into one another. Think of it as a waterfall effect, as one bucket fills and overflows it pours into the next bucket, allowing you to execute at a level far more efficient than if you were attempting to fill them individually. In other words, your faith will feed your family, and your family will make you better at your career, and so on. As you go down the categories, you find that one will lead to another. Once you get to charity it is not the end, charity will then feed right back into faith and here we have our continual improvement loop again where the Core Components are feeding each other. This is how the spirit, mind and body continue to make you the exceptional being you were meant to be, engaging in the 6 areas of fulfillment that truly matter in life.

Now that we know what the 6 areas of fulfillment are, we must plan five-years out and move backwards to today. This detailed plan must be descriptive and paint a mental image that is clear and unobstructed in the mind's eye. Remember, leaving anything to the mind for interpretation leaves open an opportunity for the mind to go in the wrong direction. Be very descriptive when going through these steps. Starting with faith, finish the next statement as clearly and precisely as you can.

Faith

In five years, I will have achieved a level of faith I have never before achieved in the past. The level of fulfillment and power that it gives me is unmistakable. The specific things about my faith that have improved and the milestones I have reached over the past years are proof of my progress. I humbly recognize that I am better for it. It all started when I _____

_____

_____ *(remember this has yet to happen, but be descript as if it already has occurred) and the moments along the way where I stopped to look back and witness the improvement of my faith, and humbly thank the Holy Spirit for His guidance were* __

_____

_____. *It proved to me that faith is a major component of fulfillment, and I know that my spirit, mind and body are acting in unison to provide the most fulfilled life that I can have, so that I can focus on giving back to this universe that has provided me so much. The three things about my faith that I am most thankful for and will continue to nurture are* _____, _____ *and*

_____. *These three areas of my life will continue to feed me with an abundant source of energy and contentment that will satisfy my need to give back to the other 5 areas of fulfilment.*

Family

In five years I will have a rich family life that transcends anything I imagined. The level of fulfillment and power that it gives me is unmistakable, and the specific things about my family that have improved, and the milestones I have reached over the past years are proof of my progress, and I humbly recognize that I am better for it. It all started when I _____

_____ _____ *(remember this has yet to happen, but be descript as if it has already occurred). The moments along the way where I stopped to look back and witness the rich deep connection that I have with my family and humbly thank the Holy Spirit for His guidance were*

_____ _____. *It proved to me that my family is a major component of fulfillment and I know that my spirit, mind and body are acting in unison to provide the most fulfilled life that I can have, so that I may focus on giving back to this universe that has provided me so much. The three things I am most thankful for and will continue to nurture to improve the family bond and rich experience that we all currently share are* _____, _____ *and* _____, *and these three areas of my life will continue to feed me with an abundant source of energy and contentment that will satisfy my need to give back to the other 5 areas of fulfilment.*

Career

I recognize that my faith and my family are major components of living a rich and fulfilled life. Progressing in both of these areas of

121

fulfillment is necessary in order to impact my career and continue to sharpen the focus on the 'why' of my vocation. In 5 years I will have achieved a new and more advanced status, and a level that I have never before achieved in the past will soon be reached. The level of fulfillment and power that it gives me is unmistakable, and the specific things about my career that have improved and the milestones that I reached over the past years are proof of my progress. I humbly recognize that I am better for it. It all started when I _____

_____

_____ *(remember this has yet to happen, but be descript as if it has already happened) and the moments along the way where I stopped to look back and witness the positive outcomes within in my career, and humbly thank the Holy Spirit for His guidance were*

_____

_____*. It proved to me that faith and family are major components of fulfillment, and I know that my spirit, mind and body are acting in unison to provide the most fulfilled life that I can have, so that I may focus on giving back to the universe that has provided me so much. The three skills that I am most thankful for and will continue to hone are* _____, _____ *and* _____*. These three skills are necessary for continual improvement within my career, and are gifts to me from the Holy Spirit. I will continue to use the abundant source of energy that exists to find higher levels of execution so that the success that follows is unmistakable. This will ultimately enhance the feelings of fulfillment in my life and will feed my need to give back to the other 5 areas of fulfilment.*

Financial

Let's be honest with one another here. Money cannot buy happiness or fulfilment or legacy, but it sure does make it easier to focus on that which could provide many of those things. One of my close friends from high school said once, "Money can't buy happiness, but it can rent it from time to time." While I find this comical, it bears some truth... I digress.

The concept of money not buying happiness can't be ignored. You can have money, but if the other 5 areas of fulfillment are completely out of alignment, then it truly won't matter. Like the section on nutrition and the body, the financial side of fulfilment has more to do with discipline than any of the other 5 areas, because as we know we are bombarded with messages of instant gratification. Instant gratification is fast, feeds our weak body and then typically leaves us empty. Money is a means to an end, but too many people misuse it, and what is left in the balance is an unfulfilled life. In essence, money can help you fill other buckets of community and charity if you choose to, but if you squander those opportunities, you may have 'things' in your life, but you won't have the exceptional life you are seeking. Follow this exercise like the others.

I recognize that financial stability is a major component of living a rich and fulfilled life. I will have to delay gratification from time to time and follow a strict plan that allows me to have the necessities of life and in many cases those material things that allow me the opportunity to increase the efficiency of life. Money is merely a tool of fulfillment, not a measure of who or how successful I am. In five years I will have reached a level of financial well-being that allows me to focus on fulfillment and not be concerned with the pressures of financial needs to live. I will live below my means and amass a financial position that allows me to participate in community and charity only enjoyed by those who plan in that manner. My approach will be deliberate and with purpose. My financial position will provide a level of fulfillment and power that is unmistakable, and not to create a life of excess, but to share a life of abundance with those less fortunate who will in turn share with others as well. In five years I will have _____ in my emergency account because it is my responsibility to my family. I will_____

123

_____ *(remember this has
yet to happen, but be descript as if it has already happened) and the
moments along the way where I stopped to look back and witness the
positive outcomes within in my career and the decisions I made that
has given me a life of abundance were_____
_____ . I know that the
stresses of money are material, worldly stresses that will not enter into
my life. I will live well beneath my means and practice charity when
and wherever possible. I know that my spirit, mind and body are acting in unison to provide the most fulfilled life that I can have so that I
may focus on giving back to those less fortunate that are interested in
improving themselves, but just need an opportunity to do so. The three
disciplines that I will continue to hone for continual improvement of
my financial position in life are _____, _____ and
_____. These three disciplines that are gifts to me from the
Holy Spirit will continue to provide for me and my family in a manner
that will allow me to achieve an exceptional life that is as much a joy
as it is a responsibility. I will become a financial warrior for those who
need the help by providing opportunity for those that wish to improve
their position with their family and the Holy Spirit. This will ultimately
enhance the feeling of fulfillment within in my life and will feed my
need to give back to the other 5 areas of fulfilment.*

Community

Seeking out relationships within your own community is essential to fulfillment because the community truly is the local version of
your universal power. The power of others wanting and striving for
your fulfillment will enhance your ability to obtain it. If you are doing
good work for your community others will want this for you so you
may continue. Finding ways to serve your community is the first step
in achieving this and it is amazing how community minded people
become the 'go to' people in situations where stewardship and leadership is needed. It is an unmistakable way of creating a legacy. Start

small! Your neighborhood is in need of attention! Provide that attention and watch your importance, value and purpose grow within your community. Keep in mind, this is not to feed your ego and if this is something that you struggle with it can easily get you out of alignment with what you are called to do. Understand that value is created when you can do for others, not for yourself. You are only important to the community when you provide for the community, not when the community provides for you. Remember, you are strong and you seek to provide opportunity that seeks the same abundant life that you currently have. Community watch programs, beautification programs or something as simple as picking up trash on the roadside within the community with a group of your neighbors are all ways to improve community and enhance relationships along the way. Remember that our mindfulness needs those relationships to grow, and mindfulness allows us to live in the moment and enjoy all that has been provided.

I recognize that my community is a major component in living a rich and fulfilled life. Providing for my community and seeking out relationships within it is necessary for me to grow as a person and achieve a high level of fulfillment within my life. In 5 years I will have achieved a new and more advanced status in my community, a status that has never before been achieved by me in the past. The level of fulfillment and power that it gives me is unmistakable. It all started when I _____

_____ (remember this has yet to happen, but be descript as if it has already happened) and the moments along the way where I stopped to look back and witness the positive outcomes that were created through this were_____

___.

_____

_____ . It proved to me that relationships within my community are major components of fulfillment and I know that my spirit, mind and body are acting in unison to provide the most fulfilled life that I can have so that I may focus on giving back *to the universe that has provided me so much. The three things that I can point to where I have made a positive impact over the past five years are _____, _____ and _____. These three outcomes that are gifts to me from the Holy Spirit will continue to impact the community in a manner that will outlive me and my time on earth. This ultimately provides a feeling of fulfillment in my life and will feed my need to continue to seek out these important relationships in my community and give back to the other 5 areas of fulfilment.*

Charity

When considering charity, I have to quote my mother who once said, "Charity starts at home," and what she meant by that is that there are certain family issues that must be taken care of before we can help others. Board any flight and they tell you, "If cabin pressure should be lost, you place the oxygen over your mouth and nose first, then help others." This is the same for charity! Take care of the other 5 areas of fulfillment, and charity not only becomes easy, it becomes far more rewarding. Don't get me wrong, I am not asking you to provide your family with massive amounts of worldly goods, and then give a dollar to the United Way. I am telling you that the needs of your family supersede the needs of the public, because you are first and foremost responsible for them. If your daughter has a flat tire and you want to go and feed the homeless, go fix your daughter's flat tire, then both of you can drive to help the homeless. That is how this works! Humility and charity are two of the best ways to find complete alignment with the Holy Spirit, and this works both personally and professionally.

One of the core values at TekLinks, a regional systems integration company where currently I serve as their Chief Operations Officer, has as one of their core values, "Serve the Community." The rewards that we have experienced through this endeavor to serve go beyond the schools we have adopted and the charities we have supported over the years. It has brought us closer to the communities we serve and actually increased business. This is because as a group we have aligned ourselves with the communities that we serve, and those communities give back, in a very positive way. Charity helps those in need and absolutely gives back to the giver! Let's work from the template.

In five years I will have achieved a level of fulfillment in my family that will allow me to focus on charity for others. The level of fulfillment and power that it gives me is unmistakable, and the specific things about my acts of charity that have improved and the milestones I have reached over the past few years are proof of my progress, and I humbly recognize that I am better for it. It all started when I _____

_____ *(remember this has yet to happen, but be descript as if it has already happened) and the moments along the way where I stopped to look back and witness the charitable things that I have accomplished were so incredibly rewarding that it almost seemed as if I were doing them for my own immediate family. I humbly thank the Holy Spirit for His guidance as he showed me that charity can provide me fulfillment. The most rewarding charitable project I worked on this year was*_____

_____. *It proved to me that charity is a major component of fulfillment, and I know that my spirit, mind and body are acting in unison to provide the most fulfilled life that I can have, so that I may focus on giving back to the universe that has provided me so much.*

In our next chapters we will look more deeply at the three-year plan, the one-year plan and then break that year into quarterly accomplishments and weekly tasks. As you will see, the five-year plan provides only direction, and the three year and one year plans are more activity specific. Incidentally, this is not just a great way to plan and track your exceptional life, The Enhanced Corporate Performance process for business will enhance your focus and channel energy for you and your staff in a direction that leads to employee autonomy and fulfillment. In today's competitive landscape, having employees that you can depend on as extraordinary producers adds immeasurable value. I suggest to all of my corporate clients to complete the Enhanced Life Performance program first, and then complete the Corporate Performance Program as a team. Finally, if you are an executive in that company, the Enhanced Executive Program is an ongoing system that helps coach busy executives to execute at the highest possible levels through the proper prioritization of core responsibilities, while creating the best version of self!

Continual Improvement – The five-year plan should be reviewed at every quarterly deep dive that is part of the Enhanced Life Continual Improvement Plan. Remember, we are not just going to let life happen to us, we are going to align ourselves with that which we are meant to become, then track and measure our effectiveness as we execute. As stated in the book *Living Forward* by Michael Hyatt and Daniel Harkavy, too many of us are drifting through our lives as spectators, reacting to our circumstances. Measurement is key to making sure we are on the proper path. There is an old saying that says that 'we measure what matters' and in this case, what could matter more than living an extraordinary life?

CHAPTER 9

The Three and One-Year Plan

"It does not do to leave a live dragon out of your calculations,
if you live near him."
—J.R.R. Tolkien, The Hobbit

I ABSOLUTELY LOVE this quote! Mr. Tolkien understands the need for detail planning in our life. Are you considering the live dragons that you live by? There are more live dragons than you know, and we will discuss how to avoid them and more importantly, how not to become one yourself.

Before moving on, make sure you have completed the steps in Chapter 7, because you can't create a detailed three-year, one-year and quarterly plan without knowing where your target is. The three-year plan will become much more detailed than just a listing of goals. Within each category, we will list at least three key initiatives that you will embark on to improve your current position.

Faith, Family, Career, Financial, Community and Charity are all areas of our life that we seek fulfillment in, and using these categories allows us to have a full view of what we are trying to accomplish. Keep in mind that 3 key initiatives multiplied times 6 areas of fulfilment would equal 18 initiatives that need to be considered. This will look daunting at first, especially if you are deficient in all of these 6 areas. While some may experience a deficiency in a large number of these areas, it is not likely that you aren't experiencing some sort of fulfillment in one or more of them. If you feel unfulfilled in all areas, don't get frustrated or upset with yourself, this is what this process is for and it accounts for those of us who feel like there is nothing fulfilling in life. As you likely know, a life with no fulfillment is dangerous, and is in the prime positon to be utilized by evil to bring others down. Obviously, this is the last thing you want. If you take some time to think, you know people like this. Everything they say or do is shrouded in negativity; they are basically live dragons that live around you. Their lives are miserable and it is everybody else's fault but their own, and if that isn't negative enough, they will also be glad to help you understand that your success is sheer luck and maybe you don't really deserve it. Please don't listen to these people, and for God's sake don't become one of them. So before moving on, look in the mirror and truly be honest to seek out where in your life you have become the live dragon. I have encountered people who are only harboring these feelings in one or two areas of their lives. If in your review you find that negativity reigns supreme, you must address this by asking the Holy Spirit to rid you of evil, and boldly ask that this evil move on, because you have made a conscious decision to evict evil from your life.

Once you have recommitted to the positive energy of the Holy Spirit and the universe, our next step would be to ascertain where we are with each area of fulfillment and then decide how we wish to maintain or improve that position. This is not an evaluation of negativity, but an improvement exercise, and as we know there is always room for improvement. It is acceptable within your three-year plan to focus on the areas that are deficient before addressing improvement in areas that are already providing a fulfilling position, so do try and focus on those areas that need the most help.

You will find, much like in the last chapter that we will use a very specific process, and it will require a clear heart and mind. In our coaching, this process of planning takes a minimum of two days, and for others it might take even longer. Please don't be discouraged if you find this difficult to complete, it is supposed to be. After all, if this was easy, you and for that matter others would have already done it. Keep in mind that for the first 5 years of my professional career, I knew this program was within my grasp and I still couldn't find it. I had a supernatural knowledge that this heightened sense of consciousness existed, but it took an alarming amount of concentration, meditation and prayer to get me where this program is today. If you are struggling with this, especially in the beginning, then you are probably on the right track. I will say again, just because I have created and use this methodology, doesn't mean that even I get it right all the time. This takes practice and will be difficult at first. I can promise you this, many of the outcomes are lasting, so even as you vacillate back and forth between executing this program at a high level and not, improvement will persist.

Let's move on and start down the path of the three-year plan. The examples below are real and are part of my plan. Keep in mind this is my personal plan, and I would never ask anyone to openly share their plan with the rest of the world unless you wanted to. I will caution you that once you use this program and it has positively impacted your life, you will want to teach others, and honestly there is no better way for you and I to leave a legacy than to pass on the power and grace of this program.

The three-year plan starts with a statement that should level set where you are in that one area of the 6 areas of fulfilment:

Faith — Today my faith is strong and my love for God and my savior Jesus Christ is deep and meaningful. The Holy Spirit interacts regularly in my life. He speaks to me and sometimes through me as I contemplate how best to serve Him and my community, friends and family. As a humble servant and passionate warrior I ask you to guide me and show me an unobstructed view of the path before me.

As I mentioned, this is a general level set statement that says, 'Here is where I am and here is what I need from the Holy Spirit,' the next statement will provide the focused key initiatives that you will utilize to improve your position.

I find that my strength in faith is tested regularly and my ability to remain positive and focused on the word to be a challenge. I know to be congruent with the Holy Spirit, I must continue to seek out humility and keep my own ego in check. Reading the word is essential to maintain that level of humility and a humble servant mentality that is necessary to leave a legacy. Material things provide me nothing here on earth or in the next life. Lastly, while I don't wear my faith on my sleeve or preach to others, I need to feel more comfortable sharing my testimony and letting others know how powerful the Holy Spirit can be in their lives.

Keeping the level set statements in mind, I list these three key initiatives for my three-year plan.

- *Read the Word – There is no excuse not to read the one book that truly sets the tone for how we should lead our lives. God does not change and nor does the true nature of mankind. For this reason, the bible can set the truth in perspective even in times when things seem so out of sync with the rest of the universal powers that the Holy Spirit commands. I will be engaged in a bible study with men who share similar mindsets, and some who challenge me to go further in my faith!*

  » *How will I measure my success? I want to have a deep understanding of the word and I must be in the word to do so. I will achieve the following:*

    I will read from the bible daily and my three-year plan is to have joined a bible study that both informs and challenges me to have a deeper relationship with The Holy Spirit and His word. I will track daily my task of reading the bible, and at the end of each quarter measure whether I am achieving what I had hoped from the bible study.

- *Share my testimony – I have always been relatively private when it comes to my faith. I will purposefully seek out people who need to be exposed to the word and share my testimony with those who need to hear it.*

» *How will I measure success? In order to share my testimony, I must be in a position to do so at the right place and right time. I will record each time I have made a connection with someone spiritually and strive to have accomplished this at least 3 times per quarter.*

- *Increase my focus on Jesus' message of humility – Often times I lose sight of why I achieve at the level that I do. It is not because of me; it is because the Holy Spirit allows me to do so. Keeping this message of humility is difficult for me because I depend on what I think of as 'my will.' Or 'my discipline.' Neither of these attributes are mine to own, they are gifts from the Holy Spirit and I will continue to thank Him for these gifts.*

  » *How will I measure success? In my daily reading I will always end with giving thanks to the Holy Spirit for the gifts He has given me, ask for forgiveness when I have allowed my ego to tell me that I am anything without God, and ask for guidance when showing others to be confident and never quit seeking the legacy that we wish to be. At each quarterly legacy review I will evaluate my prayer and meditation sessions and verify that thankfulness and humility is the strongest focus in each.*

Now you can see how the three-year plan begins to take shape and actually creates a step-based process of how we will achieve this heightened level of consciousness and measure our effectiveness. I have already defined at least two daily tasks that are a part of my life today. This is how the three-year plan feeds into the one year, the legacy quarterly review and the daily task list. There is a template of the three-year plan in the appendix and available for download from the www.enhancedlifeperformance.com website. Members of our ELP monthly high performers may also receive a completed version of my 5, 3, 1 and daily task plan so that you may compare to your own, but I would suggest that you contact one of our coaches or utilize someone who has gone through our program to help you through the process. It does take some discipline to remain focused and stay on track. If you would like to talk to one of our coaches, feel free to contact me at dmonistere@enhancedlifeperformance.com

I will stick with my example of the faith component and show you how we will be more descriptive in the one-year plan. Remember the goal. This is a 'Legacy Plan' it is acceptable to set goals that seem difficult for you to accomplish today. These goals will become easier to accomplish once you become engaged in the process and it is all written down in front of you in your Legacy Plan, giving you a clear concise, unobstructed view of what you need to accomplish to achieve legacy.

The One-Year Plan

Let's get started on the one-year Plan. We begin with a statement that will allow a focus on each key initiative in the 'Faith' area of fulfilment.

This year I will accomplish many things, in the fulfillment area of 'Faith.' I will focus on three key initiatives which include reading the word, sharing my testimony and remaining humble in times where confidence and command are needed. I will achieve this because my plan is a focused approach to leaving a legacy after I am gone.

- **The single most important thing that I wish to achieve this year in the key initiative of reading the word is first to utilize the book,** *Power Thoughts Devotional***, by Joyce Meyer, to read daily and, at the end of each week, spend 15 minutes researching the power thoughts of the week.**

» *I will measure that I am effective in this endeavor by placing it as one of my 'quick hits' tasks (more on this later) so that I know I must accomplish it each day. In my quarterly 'Legacy Review' I will track how often I missed and make improvement if needed.*

- *The single most important thing that I wish to achieve this year in the key initiative of sharing my testimony is to take the opportunity when I feel the moment is right to share my testimony and trials that I have gone through to seek a deeper connection with the community that I serve. I realize that some attempts will not create that spiritual connection that I seek, but it is my goal to do so at least 3 times per quarter.*

  » *I will measure my effectiveness to see if between each Legacy Plan Review that I have made a deep spiritual connection at least three times. I understand that in order to reach this goal I may have to attempt this more than ten or fifteen times in a quarter which must be tracked. If I have not reached three deep spiritual connections I will increase the number of times I will attempt it.*

- *The single most important thing that I wish to achieve this year in the key initiative of remaining humble and practicing humility is to not be defensive or seek out excuses or explanations when someone is asking me to change the way that I approach something, or when they are criticizing how I have behaved. All too often, great advice is given and I choose not to hear it because I am not approaching the conversation with humility. I will remain mindful that even though not all criticism is constructive, there is something within that person's word that I need to own.*

  » *I will in my quarterly Legacy Plan Review track the number of times that I have committed to approach a situation differently. I will record this in my daily task sheet in the legacy portion of the sheet and study it during my Legacy Plan Review.*

As you can see, this gets to be much more detailed as you go. The measurement and the review process is what you will be doing each quarter. This quarterly Legacy Plan Review is crucial to the success of your Legacy Plan and will be detailed in the next chapter. It will allow you to refocus your attention and help you succeed in your one-year and five-year plan.

As you go through this process for all of the areas of fulfilment: Faith, Family, Career, Financial, Community and Charity, you will begin to see patterns emerge and a much more descriptive view of what it will be like to live this enhanced life that has a specific purpose. You will not be meandering through life any longer, you will be focused and purpose driven. The one thing that I will caution you here is that when you are done, the plan will seem insurmountable, as if you couldn't possibly accomplish all that you have written down. I would suggest to you that if you have been trying to live a life of fulfillment, you are probably doing more "activities" than even the plan will have; it just isn't focused or prepared with purpose. This methodology of living sharpens the blade if you will. It brings your purpose and attempts at a fulfilled life in to focus, a clear unobstructed view of exactly what you should be doing.

To use a sports analogy, if you were playing 7 on 7 football, the old way of life would be like getting in the huddle and asking your finely tuned, highly skilled players to just run around and get open so you can throw them the ball. Sure, it will work from time to time, but wouldn't it be better if all six of the guys—who are awesome at what they do-had a specific route to run that was designed to get them in an open part of the field? Wouldn't that increase the chances of the pass being completed? Unless you just suck as a quarterback, life gets really easy. I digress…

Last Step

The last step of the process goes like this: under each statement that you have created that illustrates the single most important thing that you need to accomplish, you need to list the human, mechanical, monetary, emotional, spiritual, mental and physical resources that you will need to accomplish this key initiative. In essence, we are listing the things that you have to obtain in order to carry out this initiative.

Whether it is your wife, your husband, your boss or your brother, list the people and any other resources that you will need to engage to accomplish these initiatives. At some point the things we call on in our lives, communities and our mind become the support system that aids us in accomplishing fulfillment, or become the hurdles that get in our way that forces us down another path. Remember, evil is not interested in you becoming this good at anything, especially when your 'good' becomes helpful to others. Be mindful of what that looks like and be prepared to do battle. It is our responsibility to put ourselves in the best position to give back to the universe, and we have to do that from a position of strength, not weakness.

As an example of this I present the following:

- *The single most important thing that I wish to achieve this year in the key initiative of reading the word is first to utilize the book,* **Power Thoughts Devotional,** *by Joyce Meyer, to read daily and at the end of each week spend 15 minutes researching the power thoughts of the week and spending more time in the word looking at how the various texts treat each of those thoughts.*
  - » *I will measure that I am effective in this endeavor by placing it as one of my 'quick hits' tasks so that I know I must accomplish it each day. In my quarterly 'Legacy Review' I will track how often I missed and make improvement if needed.*
  - » *Resources Needed: my bible (at home and at work),*

community bible study group, my wife, my children, community with the Holy Spirit, spiritual strength, discipline, time (well-planned schedule) my daily task list, and my mental faculties to comprehend what the word means to me.

This is a good example of how it works, and once you complete the three and one-year plan, the daily and weekly tasks become far easier to create because you have a much better view of the target and the things you need to do to hit it.

CHAPTER 10

Five-year Plan- Revisited

"All you need is the plan, the road map,
and the courage to press on to your destination."
-Earl Nightingale

AS WE MENTIONED, it is now appropriate to look at the broader statements that we made when we considered our five-year plan. As you recall, I gave a template that detailed the broad information you would need when addressing the 6 areas of fulfillment. Keep in mind, one or two of the six areas of fulfillment may mean little to you, but they can't be ignored. The five-year plan is a target and should give you very broad goals that are directionally accurate and with very deep meaning, but they shouldn't be the directions themselves. If one of the 6 areas of fulfillment is of little concern for whatever reason, focus in on other areas, but please do not skip it. Below you will see my five-year broad plan for **Faith** written out utilizing the template that I provided:

Faith

In five years, I will have achieved a level of faith I have never before achieved in the past. The level of fulfillment and power that it gives me is unmistakable. The specific things about my faith that have improved and the milestones I have reached over the past years are proof of my progress. I humbly recognize that I am better for it. It all started when I focused in on my Legacy Plan and made a focused effort to accept the Holy Spirit and engage Him in prayer and the moments along the way where I stopped to look back and witness the improvement of my faith, and humbly thank the Holy Spirit for His guidance were when I left encounters with friends and family and openly discussed how my faith was guiding me and the heightened awareness to God's presence in and around me was helping me to become a better person. It proved to me that faith is a major component of fulfillment, and I know that my spirit, mind and body are acting in unison to provide the most fulfilled life that I can have, so that I can focus on giving back to this universe that has provided me so much. The three things about my faith that I am most thankful for and will continue to nurture are my new found openness, the strength and focus it has brought me and more importantly the grace that I am granted. These three areas of my life will continue to feed me with an abundant source of energy and contentment that will satisfy my need to give back to the other five areas of fulfilment.

This is my example of my broad five-year plan. It touches on areas of my life that my three-year and one-year plan leads to and will help me to achieve.

In the last chapter we pulled our epitaph, T-shirt slogan and listed the resources that we would need in order to accomplish our one-year plan. This allows us to take a long hard look at who we are today. We will need to do this again once we start mapping out our daily tasks, but if we pull all of this information together we will see a very detailed plan coming into picture.

So let's compile all that we have for my one and three-year plans. We can begin to create a synopsis of where we want to be in the fifth year, using the template as the opening statement and then a broader statement about each step in the one and three-year plan.

First let's compile all that we need for the one and three-year plan:

I find that my strength in faith is tested regularly and my ability to remain positive and focused on the word to be a challenge. I know to be congruent with the Holy Spirit I must continue to seek out humility and keep my own ego in check. Reading the word is essential to maintaining that level of humility and humble servant mentality that is necessary to leave a legacy. Material things provide me nothing here on earth or in the next life. Lastly, while I don't wear my faith on my sleeve or preach to others, I need to feel more comfortable sharing my testimony and letting others know how powerful the Holy Spirit can be in their lives.

Keeping this in mind, I list these three key initiatives for my three-year plan.

- *Read the Word – There is no excuse not to read the one book that truly sets the tone for how we should lead our lives. God does not change and nor does the true nature of mankind. For this reason, the bible can set the truth in perspective even in times when things seem so out of sync with the rest of the universal powers that the Holy Spirit commands. I will be engaged in a bible study with men who share similar mind sets and some who challenge me to go further in my faith!*

  » *How will I measure my success? I want to have a deep understanding of the word and I must be in the word to do so. I will achieve the following:*

    I will read from the bible daily and my three-year plan is to have joined a bible study that both informs and challenges me to have a deeper relationship with the Holy Spirit and His word. I will track daily my task of reading the bible and at the end of each quarter measure whether I am achieving what I had hoped from the bible study.

  » *Resources Needed: my bible (at home and at work), community bible study group, my wife, my children, community with the Holy Spirit, spiritual strength, discipline, time (well-planned schedule) my daily task list, and my mental faculties to comprehend what the word means to me.*

- *Share my testimony – I have always been relatively private when it comes to my faith. I will purposefully seek out people who need to be exposed to the word and share my testimony with those who need to hear it.*

  » *How will I measure success? In order to share my testimony, I must be in a position to do so at the right place and right time. I will record each time I have made a connection with someone spiritually and strive to have accomplished this at least 3 times per quarter.*

  » *Resources Needed: my confidence, my wife, my children, community with the Holy Spirit, spiritual strength, discipline, my daily task list and a desire to impact others.*

- *Increase my focus on Jesus' message of humility – Often times I lose sight of why I achieve at the level that I do. It is not because of me, it is because the Holy Spirit allows me to do so. Keeping this message of humility is difficult for me because I depend on what I think of as 'my will.' Or 'my discipline.' Neither of these attributes is mine to own, they are gifts from the Holy Spirit and I will continue to thank Him for these gifts.*

  » *How will I measure success? In my daily reading I will always end with giving thanks to the Holy Spirit for the gifts He has given me, ask for forgiveness when I have allowed my ego to tell me that I am anything without God, and ask for guidance when showing others to be confident and never quit seeking the legacy that we wish to be. At each quarterly legacy review I will evaluate my*

*prayer and meditation sessions and verify that thankful-
ness and humility is the strongest focus in each.*

» **Resources Needed: my bible (at home and at work),
   Mother Teresa's humility list, Practice using the word we
   more than I. The book "Ego is the Enemy"**

Obviously, you can see this gets very detailed and if you are keeping these notes precisely having a binder and using it as a reference
throughout the year is a great way to execute the plan. You will see in
the next chapters how the daily tasks will help accomplish this but it
is good to leaf through this document regularly.

Now that I have compiled all of this information I can use the
template provided and have all I need to create a broad directionally
accurate statement for my five-year plan. The five-year plan section
for Faith would look like this

Five-year plan - Faith

*In five years, I will have achieved a level of faith I have never
before achieved in the past. The level of fulfillment and power that it
gives me is unmistakable. The specific things about my faith that have
improved and the milestones I have reached over the past years are
proof of my progress. I humbly recognize that I am better for it. It all
started when I focused in on my Legacy Plan and made a focused
effort to accept the Holy Spirit and engage Him in prayer and the
moments along the way where I stopped to look back and witness
the improvement of my faith, and humbly thank the Holy Spirit for
His guidance were when I left encounters with friends and family and
openly discussed how my faith was guiding me and the heightened
awareness to God's presence in and around me was helping me to
become a better person. It proved to me that faith is a major component of fulfillment, and I know that my spirit, mind and body are
acting in unison to provide the most fulfilled life that I can have, so*

143

that I can focus on giving back to this universe that has provided me so much. The three things about my faith that I am most thankful for and will continue to nurture are <u>my new found openness,</u> <u>the strength and focus it has brought me</u> and <u>more importantly the grace that I am granted</u>. These three areas of my life will continue to feed me with an abundant source of energy and contentment that will satisfy my need to give back to the other five areas of fulfilment.

In order to find fulfillment of Faith, I will Focus on Jesus' message of humility and surround myself with His word. All things can be achieved through the Father, the Son and the Holy Spirit and the Word will be my guide.

As you can see the broad statement above says what we will do, but does not have individual action steps. This is something you can put at the top of your daily task page and as you carry out your daily tasks you will find that it is in line with what you choose to accomplish long term. Having created the three and one-year plan allowed us to make the five-year plan more accurate and based off of the very steps that it will take to achieve the goals you seek.

The Legacy Plan Quarterly Review – As we have discussed, reviewing your plan needs to be done quarterly. This will not be a detailed deep dive; it is a check and verification that we are on the proper path. The review is a simple three step process: Did you hit the goal? Did the goal meet its intended outcome? How can you improve it? Using the goal of my intent to improve on public prayer, this is a snippet taken directly from one of my quarterly reviews:

Did you hit your goal? Please explain: *After reviewing the past quarter, I found that public prayer was not an easy task for me to complete at first. Once I was accepting of the fact that our goal for public prayer is never to be perfect or to seek approval from the people that might be in the room, I found this to be much easier. This goal was created in an attempt to increase my own level of humility, but I fear that the confidence it has created within me is not truly humble and more about the acceptance of men. I don't need that acceptance and this is counter to a humble approach. I am not ready to remove this* *item from this category or remove it all together, but I will be more mindful that my public prayer should be an attempt to stir emotion in others instead of an increase in confidence of public speaking for me.*

Did this goal stir something in you emotionally? Please explain: *This did stir something emotionally within me, but I will admit not necessarily a spiritual impact as others might think, it was more my own public confidence.*

What can be added or taken away to increase the effectiveness or improve? *As mentioned above, I must remember what the goal was created for and remain humble in my approach to conquer a fear of public prayer. I need to make sure that my prayer is aimed at helping others, not making me feel comfortable with the way others might think of me. It is not a performance, it is an emotional prayer.*

Continual Improvement – This is a great way to make sure you are in constant alignment with your long term goals. Five years, regardless of your age is a lifetime. It goes by fast, but to look out five years and say I want to do this or that, is difficult. This is why so few people actually plan their lives. The continual improvement step is built in. If you find that your daily tasks do not fall in line with this five-year goal, then it is time to evaluate where your Legacy Plan has gone astray. While I feel the Legacy Plan can be utilized by both men and women, I would argue that men need this more than women, because the temptation of man to only do the minimum amount required to get by seems to be rampant in our society today. Men are depicted on television as ignorant, lazy and unreliable, and I tell you that this and other factors are beginning to negatively impact the men in our society. Men should begin to hold themselves to a higher standard. I am not one to suggest that women are inferior and they need our help, but I will say that we are, for the most part physically stronger when it comes to handling various physical and emotional stressors of life, and we have failed our children and the women of this time. Women are incredibly proficient at everything they do, and for the most part it has been out of necessity because men have shirked this responsibility. As I mentioned in my mission statement, there are

145

too few real men in this world, I implore you to become one and to teach your sons how to be real men as well. I look at the number of men who brutalize their wives or significant others and it is obvious that we have failed.

CHAPTER **11**

Weekly and Daily Tasks

"Planning is bringing the future into the present
so that you can do something about it now."
—*Alan Lakein, writer*

THE WEEKLY AND daily tasks worksheet is how we take all of the information that we have gathered in this process and put it into daily execution. Remember all the planning is for nothing if we don't take the information and act on it.

Before I move on, please remember that whether you are doing this in written format or electronically, never throw these weekly and daily task sheets away. Remember that our execution is only the second step in the, 'Plan, Execute, Evaluate, Improve' process. In order to take inventory of our week and the execution of our day, the last two steps are the ones that lead us to the extraordinary life we seek. Evaluation does two things. It helps you decide if you are on the right track, and if you look at your week or month over time, you start to notice trends in your life. You may find out that you do a better job of completing your tasks on days that you exercise, or you may find out that vigorous exercise leaves you without much energy for the rest of the day. Remember we discussed in the chapter on Body that energy management is key to having a great day.

Your weekly schedule should look like this:

Sunday Night — Take 15 minutes to organize the upcoming week. Set your weekly goals and set your tasks for Monday. If your daily tasks template is well laid out this should not take very long to accomplish. It isn't necessary to have every detail of every day Monday through Friday. Many of the supportive tasks will take some time to expose themselves to you in the first couple of days during that week.

Monday-Friday — At the end of each day you must prepare your tasks for the following day and evaluate your weekly progress towards the 6 areas of fulfillment. Again, be mindful of trends and do everything that you can to place yourself in the best position to be successful. I keep a pretty comprehensive food log and I have made some incredible discoveries about how my body reacts to certain foods and my overall performance throughout the week. I consider myself a bit of a biohacker, so for me tweaking the body to perform at an optimal level is a bit of a hobby and I enjoy it. All I am asking here is for you to pay attention to trends that you see as the days unfold.

Friday Afternoon — The last hour of each Friday is YOUR TIME! Make sure that you take the time to evaluate your week. See what you accomplished and record any Small Wins or Legacy Impressions. Be sure to transfer your Legacy Impressions to your Legacy Impressions tracking system so that you may review them during your quarterly review. Legacy Impressions help build momentum and further support the fact that you are on the right track.

Saturday — REST! Don't look at this at all on Saturday and allow your life to be a bit more spontaneous and off of the structured approach that you take during the week. This follows the same concepts that we discussed in previous chapters about a focused approach to our daily tasks and an aggressive attack of your day. In order to do this consistently our bodies must have an opportunity to rest. Saturday consider your rest from structure!

The brain uses more energy than any other organ in our body

and this fact further supports the necessity of having a good nutrition and meal plan. This means that not only do we have to fuel the body and mind correctly, but we must give it ample rest. This is why you should pick a day on the weekend to just be off the grid. I choose Saturday because I like to review my previous week and prepare for the upcoming week on Sunday evenings. This means my Saturdays are utilized for rest only.

I have included the template that I use for my weekly and daily tasks. Remember how we got here and you will start to tie in why the utilization of this program allows us to have an extraordinary life. Nothing is happening randomly! We are planning our lives in detail, executing our plan, evaluating the effectiveness of those daily and weekly tasks, and then making improvements to help facilitate a better outcome. The Enhanced Life Program works for corporate planning as well and starts with the Mission, Vision and Values of the company, but the plan must be detailed and strategic. If you are interested in contacting one of our coaches to lead a corporate session, please feel free to reach out to me at dmonistere@enhancedlifeperformance.com

Before moving on, I want to point out that I keep track of my weekly and daily tasks on paper. Every week I have a summary placed in my planner of the one-year plan. I review it weekly as I look back on the previous week and begin planning for the following. This way I know that my 6 areas of fulfillment and the Main, Secondary and Supportive tasks that must be done are in keeping with the one-year plan. Let's dissect the worksheet and then talk about how we tie it into the plan.

Weekly Goals and the 6 Areas of Fulfillment — As we mentioned in Chapter 7, we are tapping into a supernatural power that reaches beyond the ordinary. The 6 areas of fulfillment: Faith, Family, Career Financial, Community and Charity are core components of how we leave a legacy. With very few exceptions, these 6 areas must be addressed in order to have the incredible life we wish to have. In our 5 year plan, if we followed the template, we were very specific about what we wished to achieve, we further revised it in our one year plan. Daily, we must make sure that we are tracking the items that we must do in order to further that plan. This doesn't mean we have to have something for every area every day. I mentioned in previous chapters what I wanted to do to become more fulfilled in my faith. I must have at least one thing planned that week and if something happens spontaneous as well, I can record it here. This way in review we can better track how often we are addressing this area.

The Quick Hits — We treat the quick hits a little differently. These are things that 90% of the time we must do every day. These tasks likely don't take long or they are part of your daily routine. As you can see, exercise is one that I have listed and quite frankly, unless I am sick, I never miss. Meditation however, is something that is incredibly necessary for me, but it is one I struggle with, so the daily reminder helps me to see when I am on or off track. If I go more than two days without meditating, I force myself to stop what I am doing and meditate that very moment.

Big Task for the Day — The Big Task for the day is usually work or family related. It will likely feed your Financial, Family and Career categories of fulfillment and that is exactly what we are after. Make sure you accomplish this one task… it is your main responsibility for the day!

Secondary Tasks for the Day — Utilizing the 1,3,5 rule, these secondary tasks are usually small projects that tend to involve and depend on other people in our sphere of community influence. People we work with or have relationships with. Make sure you finish your part and find ways to remind yourself of the things others owe you. You may have to wait on others to complete the task itself, but your part needs to be completed and you must communicate with whoever you are working with that the next step is in his or her court. This will not come off of your list until they complete their phase. We focus our attention on the Big Task and we need to make sure that above all, that task is completed. The secondary tasks are just as important and need attention. We find that eighty percent of the value in the day resides in these tasks. Make sure before you move on that the 1 and 3 list of tasks are complete before you move on to the supportive tasks.

Supportive Tasks for the Day — These are smaller tasks for which you should allow yourself softer deadlines and flexibility. They are important and support the other tasks that are likely on or will soon hit your 1 and 3 list. Don't beat yourself up if you fail to complete this set of tasks, just evaluate the importance and decide if it needs to go on tomorrow's list. At some point, if ignored long enough, it could escalate to a 1 or 3 level task. You will notice that the last task is to plan tomorrow's day. Of all the supportive tasks, this is the most crucial so you can hit the ground running the next day.

Notes — You will find the notes section in the template is never big enough. I typically have an entire page set aside for notes. The way the template works is that the back side of the daily task template is an entire notes page. This way when I open my day timer, the section on the left can be used for notes. This area can be used to track anything you desire and keeps you from carrying multiple notepads throughout the day. I find that in my Friday review, many of the notes taken will lead to tasks at some point in time. This obviously is very important in your weekly planning session on Sunday. Keep in mind it is not imperative to follow this daily activity sheet to the letter. Pick and choose the concepts that work for you, but make sure you are using a methodology that leaves very little to chance. If you get out of the habit of using the tool, don't try and go back to recreate the week or God forbid the month!

Weekly Goals for the 6 areas of life fulfilment:

This week I will :

Faith-

Family-

Career-

Financial-

Community-

Charity-

Todays tasks consist of:

Quick hits:

[ ] Journal [ ] Exercise [ ] Meditate [ ] Write for 15 [ ] Birthdays [ ] Encourage Someone [ ] Website [ ] Bible

1-3-5 Rule :

Big Task for the day:

[ ]

3 tasks that must be done:

[ ]

[ ]

[ ]

5 supportive tasks:

[ ]

[ ]

[ ]

[ ]

{ } Plan tomorrow's day

Small Wins \ Legacy Impressions

Date   Daily Notes

CHAPTER 12

Putting It All Together

"If we take a step despite feeling uncomfortable,
afraid, or inadequate, our comfort zones expand.
We grow in strength and skill. What we consider normal
for us changes, sometimes radically."
—Alex & Bret Harris, Do the Hard Things

NOW YOU HAVE a complete life plan that takes into consideration all of the things that you must complete in order to leave a legacy. Remember as you review this plan, no one has ever been given an award for intentions, only actions. We will dive into this concept later.

At first glance, this probably looks overwhelming, and trust me, I get that! It did to me the first time I went through this entire process for myself. Keep in mind, when I went through this process no one showed me how to do it, and the concept of 'legacy impression' was just forming in my mind. It looked good, but I didn't know how impactful it might be. For 90 or so days after I completed the Enhanced Life Program Legacy Plan, I wasn't sure if I could complete any of it, who has that kind of time? What I didn't bank on or understand, despite my rigid discipline, was that I was wasting time waffling back and forth between competing priorities that may or may not have been moving me toward the goal that I thought I had. Since they were not written down or periodically reviewed, how would I ever know?

Anyone who has worked for a large company and witnessed departments competing against one another because they had competing goals might understand how this could derail the best laid plans. Incidentally, much like our own lives, this is one of the biggest issues plaguing companies today. If you find this book helpful, be on the lookout for my next projects: Enhanced Executive Performance and Enhanced Corporate Performance, as those books too will provide practical guides to increase performance to levels most don't realize are possible.

This takes us to the first step of the evaluation process, and I will guide you on how to put all of this together, and more importantly, how you need to begin.

Competing Goals

It is time for a three hundred and sixty degree look at the plan itself. Are their goals that are competing, and if so, how do we get them in alignment? This is such an important step, and if I had known how to do this in my teen years, my life would have been much more rewarding, especially then. It is time for me to digress, but it will be to explain how competing goals can derail a rigid disciplined lifestyle.

I have always been disciplined. There was something innate within in me that allowed me to delay gratification and often times seek out activities that others looked at as less than desirable. It likely stems from my adolescent years in middle school when I decided to not be the 'fat kid' anymore. I starved myself, which took great discipline and quite a lot of self-destructive behavior. I did not eat for 3 months and became very sick. The interesting thing was that despite the fact that in 90 days I lost 50 plus pounds, and ended up at age 13 weighing only 81 pounds, people complimented me on the weight loss. I guess I took my old carefree lifestyle where gratification was instant and attached the bullying that I experienced when I was the fat kid and felt that the pain of starvation didn't equal the pain of being bullied. In fact, the pain of starvation was followed by accolades and compliments. In my mind, suffering led to positive feedback, and self-inflicted suffering takes discipline.

I carried this to my high school years as I learned that competing goals can ruin even the best laid plans. I loved baseball, but my favorite activities included lifting weights, riding my bike long distances, and martial arts. I would lift weights Monday through Friday, but I would ride 50 miles during the week and typically would log a 75 to 100 mile ride on Sundays. Then I would train for hours in the dojo. I was a competitive bodybuilder trying to put on muscle and killing my gains by riding over 200 miles per week and doing way too much cardio. These goals are not congruent with one another. My body was too thick to win in the various cycling races that I would enter because of the intense weight lifting, and I never was able to achieve the size I needed to compete in bodybuilding at the highest level. So I was disciplined to do something that others wouldn't dream of doing, but I wasn't achieving my goals because both of those goals (competing at the highest level in bodybuilding and winning bike races) cannot be achieved at the same time. It wasn't until I was 20 that I decided to cycle in moderation and focus on qualifying for the Mr. Universe competition. Once I decided to alter the goals so that they were aligned, I met with success. Incidentally, once I qualified for Mr. Universe, I decided that I had accomplished all I desired to in bodybuilding at that time, and began my journey into triathlons. Yet again, I went from a 156 pound shredded lightweight national competitor in bodybuilding, to a 136 pound athlete competing in triathlons, because it was time for the next challenge and more importantly, it was what I wanted to do. I never competed at a national level in triathlons, but I ran in races that seven years prior, I never thought I could handle watching, much less competing in.

Once you have verified that your goals are not competing, you have to break down the various items that you have uncovered as important to you and decide how your daily routine will unfold to support those items. While I offered you an example of competing goals and what I did as a teenager to fix them, it is more likely that your goals will compete in the areas of work and personal life. You may have a goal to be the leading salesperson at your company, and also to enhance your marriage by being ever more present and available to your wife. You may find, once you map out the steps to tackle both, that these goals will compete with one another and before you begin you need to make sure that everyone (including yourself) is aware of how you will tackle that challenge. You might change the goal. Or you may sit down with your wife and let her know that there might be times that achieving the goal of being the best salesperson at your company could interfere with the time that you have available to commit to developing the relationship more effectively.

Unfolding the Day

6 areas of life fulfillment — The first step in unfolding the day is to look at your 6 areas of life fulfillment and give your daily task sheet a theme, if you will. Recognize that the daily task sheet in this area speaks to what you will do that week. You will not be able to do something in every area, but there could be a theme that week where you feel compelled to focus on one area. For instance, if we use the example of the goal to be the best salesperson in the office, but you had promised your spouse that you are committed to developing the marriage or family dynamic, each week may unfold differently. You may feel like you have not been completely present for your family as of late and you want to make sure that this is an area that you excel in this week. What you will find if you actively plan time with your family, you can address the issue of enhancing the family dynamic this week and make this a theme for the week. You may decide to do something that you enjoy with your family and incidentally you may inadvertently address three other areas of life fulfillment because you might plan activities that include Charity and possibly Community. Focus in on that this week and you have begun to master the 6 areas of life fulfillment. The real test would be to see if you can honestly impact both at the same time. You may be trying to land a new account that owns five or six local restaurants in town. Imagine the positive impact that you might have on that client if you called your contact and told him, "Hey Frank, I am always trying to be successful with my career, and I have to admit that I need to spend some family time with my girls so I wanted to take them out to eat, which restaurant in your group do you suggest and what dish do you prefer when you go there?" Wow! Your contact is thinking, here is a guy who recognizes that his family is important, and oh by the way he is going to spend money with us. He may even throw you a few gift cards. Winner! I digress…

The Quick Hits — Next you need to decide what Quick Hits that you will be doing daily to support your Legacy Plan. I would look at the Quick Hits almost as habits. This is a great place to put items that you either already habitually do, or that you would like to do consistently. A daily reminder of this is a great way to get into the habit. You can see from my list some of these could be universal and be used by others. I will tell you, if you only do one thing in this program, this is the single biggest and most impactful step in the process. Even though you may already complete this step habitually, just recognizing that these tasks are getting done and reminding you when you haven't done them as well is one of the biggest aids to my daily routine. Despite many suggesting that it isn't necessary to write things down that you know you will habitually do, you will find when it is on your list two things happen. You find out that maybe you aren't as consistent as you might think; also, I get a real charge out of checking that bad boy off the list, and due to that, I really start to gain momentum in my day. There will be days that you have some ground to make up as you go through your daily review, and the Quick Hits keep you on task. With that in mind, make sure you choose your Quick Hit items wisely.

If you find that you have chosen a Quick Hit item that you never seem to get to, don't automatically assume that it is not important and take it off the list. This is a great time to evaluate why you haven't been doing it. It obviously was important enough to list, but for whatever reason you have not been able to consistently accomplish it. Break it down one or two levels to see what is hindering you from making it happen.

For instance, Exercise – You find that more often than not, you get to the end of the day and start your commute to the gym and something turns your car in the direction of your garage instead of the gym. We all have had those days where lifting a weight or walking on a treadmill would end in someone's death, especially your trainer if you should be lucky enough to hate one, I mean have one… I digress.

In this example, it might be time to change the workout to the morning, this way the day does not suck the life out of you so much that even the car thinks you need to go home instead of the gym. Another alternative might be to set up a small home gym utilizing resistance bands. The idea here is to break this down into a more basic component, and find out why it has been difficult. If you haven't been doing it because it doesn't help you leave the legacy that you so desperately want to leave, then take it off the list and find an item that does.

The 1-3-5 — The 1-3-5 system changed my life. I actually started doing this about 11 years ago when my company got larger and more complex. I used to accomplish way more than my current list has on it, but my company was smaller and I didn't have to engage or involve anyone else in the various decisions I made during the day. Once the company got larger and I built my management team, this changed. I would often times beat myself up about not being more productive, because I place a very high value on execution, but I wasn't giving credit to the idea that involving your management team is crucial to scaling your business. I realize that this is a book on a life plan and not necessarily about corporate management, or management frameworks, but what we do in our career is part of the 6 areas of fulfillment. The 1-3-5 system is liberating in that it focuses your attention on the most important thing for the day, and then allows you some leverage and liberation to attack the next most important things in a manner that hopefully doesn't overwhelm you. I will include in the reference section a 1-3-5 system guide that you can use to help categorize the items on your list, so take a look at it when you get a chance if you are struggling with what to put on your list.

Continual Improvement — This program and the daily task list, will improve itself without much effort, but you have to start! The next chapter will speak to intentions and I wanted to say that I have purposely kept this book rated PG-13 and not R for a reason. I think it could be a great reference guide for graduating high school kids and college students, but I wanted to be a little aggressive with my speech here. Especially to the millennials that are reading. This program will not work if you don't start it. Get off your ass and start! Nobody owes you anything and nothing worth having is easy. There, now I will go back to being PG 13. Of course I'm pretty sure that really wasn't anything that would get an R rating these days anyway.

CHAPTER 13

Good Intentions
& a Place Called Hell

"The road to hell is paved with good intentions."
—Johnson, Ray, Clairvoux

ALTHOUGH MANY PEOPLE believe that Samuel Johnson should get credit for the above quote, this might not be accurate. Johnson said something close, but he was following in the footsteps of others. Robert Wilson, a news editor, provided two other sources prior to Johnson.

John Ray, in 1670, cited as a proverb, "Hell is paved with good intentions." Even earlier than that, it's been attributed to Saint Bernard of Clairvaux (1091-1153), as "Hell is full of good intentions or de-sires." Just how it got to the *road* to Hell being paved this way, and not Hell itself, we can't be sure, but one thing is. It is obvious that for a very long time our intentions to do things must not have always been followed up with action. If Saint Bernard of Clairvaux who lived between 1091 and 1153 used this as a potential teaching point, it could be said that lack of action is not a new condition of the human spirit, mind and body.

I wanted to focus an entire chapter on this premise to shine a light on the fact that laziness or lack of motivation to execute can only be one of two things. Either your plan is out of alignment with what you are supposed to be doing, or evil is trying to keep you from doing the very thing you are trying to accomplish. This is a difficult concept and knowing the difference is crucial to your ability to finish. I will tell you this, no one in the past, the present or the future will win an award or leave a legacy for what they *intended* to do. You must take action! I would suggest to you that if you have gone through the Enhanced Life Legacy Plan process completely and you feel as if the Holy Spirit truly guided you through meditation to help you clarify the things you have placed within your plan, then there is only one other thing it could be. Evil is playing on our innate ability to be lethargic and disconnected with the universe, and is convincing you that the effort is not worth the outcome.

Simply put, if you are not following your daily, weekly, quarterly and annual goals, there is something wrong with the contents of your plan, or you lack the spiritual, mental and bodily strength to keep evil out of it and stay on task. If you need another round to go through your plan and ensure it is in line with what you are supposed to be doing, you must apply a humble approach to being led to the right plans, goals, tasks and endeavors in your life. We have discussed the importance of humility, and this is a perfect place to call on that humility and ask to be led instead of trying to actively do it yourself. Fill yourself with humble thoughts of love and thankfulness, and evil will have to take a back seat as you review your plan.

Many people that I come into contact with have seen my daily worksheet and have become witness to me referring to it throughout the day. I always share with them how I approach my day, and they always ask me for a copy of the template. I have never turned anyone down, but the template is only a very small part of the process. Just yesterday this happened and my work colleague blew me away! He asked me for a copy and I told him that I would be happy to provide it, but in order for it to truly be 'owned' by him he had to—. Before I could even finish, he said, "Make sure it is in line with what my goals, dreams and aspirations are." I told him that I knew that the template was in good hands and I would be happy to send it to him! The issue here is that we need to make sure that the human, logical brain is not interfering with what the Holy Spirit is asking us to do. We do this so often and the result is that we spend more time intending to do something instead of acting on it.

Place a High Value on Execution

"While others were dreaming about it – I was getting it done."
—Nathan W. Morris

Now that we have reviewed our plan and we feel we are in alignment, in order to move forward we need to execute the plan. Too many people will over evaluate and never execute. A plan that hasn't been executed is merely a dream or an intention. If while planning you feel in your heart you know you will never do what is on the page, why put it down. We are looking for small wins that will lead to bigger wins! Those bigger wins will lead to fulfillment that will put you in a position to give back which will lead to a legacy impression! Collecting multiple legacy impressions will ultimately lead to legacy!

Let's talk about what helps us to be masters of executing the plan! Before we begin discussion in this area, one of the most important things here is to just start! If you have never attempted to run your life in this manner it will be difficult to get started and difficult to make it habit. Most times we wait until we think the process is perfect. We are focused on the process and not the execution. Don't wait for perfection! As long as you feel like you have created this plan with the guidance of the Holy Spirit, it is perfect! Trust me when I tell you it has taken me 20 years to get this program where it is today, and every year I tweak it a little to improve it. What I do today does not even resemble how I started this twenty years ago. So for the love of everything that is good and Holy, just start... I digress.

In the book, *Extreme Ownership,* by Jocko Willink and Leif Babin, the authors talk about a number of things that follow along these lines. The novel is powerful and I dare say being a navy seal in a combat situation leaves little room for error and the preparation to perfect their plans is very intense. They must act when given the opportunity and they have to execute with the team as it is at that moment. They can't stop combat operations asking to run through it one more time. This book has taught me a lot, especially about team building and business management, but it can be used for life planning as well. We 'own' our plan and regardless of what gets us off track, we are ultimately responsible for that plan. Extreme Ownership of our plan is required!

The most important part of the Enhanced Life Performance program with regard to execution is the daily/weekly task list. There is a bit of art to the task list and how you create it. You will find the better you are at the task list, the better chance you have of actually getting things on the list done. We are going to go through some recommendations on the task list that will likely make a huge difference in how effective you are.

Start with something significant first — When you do something significant first each day, it is going to be hard, take a lot of energy and likely may not be fun. Doing this first does many things to set up a great day. First, you are not dreading doing the task all day long; second, completing a difficult task early builds momentum for completing the rest of your tasks more easily. Think of it as a roller coaster. The initial effort to get started is like climbing the first big hill on a roller coaster. Once you climb it and start to go downhill, the rest of the day gets easier. Granted, staying on task is essential so make sure you refer to your daily task list throughout the day.

Capture your tasks effectively – When writing your tasks, make sure you are doing so in a manner that promotes action. Make sure you use verbs to describe the task. These signal your mind and body that it's time to move and get into action mode. Make sure you have enough detail so you are setting a starting position, a path of execution and a method of completion. Lastly, if the task will take multiple days and be carried over during the week, give yourself a deadline even if you are unsure how long it might take you.

Remove hurdles and clear to neutral – Sometimes I notice that a task will get carried over from day to day due to some hurdle. It needs to get done, but for some reason, I just can't get started. Usually, this means there is something that needs to be completed before you can get the task done. For example, the task might be 'go to the eye doctor.' Let's assume you are new in town and don't know who to go to. Since you are unclear who to go to and you really weren't impressed by the google search you did, you may find that when you see this on the list, your mind thinks about the troubles of finding a good doctor as opposed to how to execute the task. You should change the task to, 'Talk to your peer group about who they recommend as a great eye doctor.' Getting this information first will help you gather the information necessary in order to knock out the task you originally set. This way the next time, 'go to the eye doctor' shows up as a task, you know exactly what needs to be done to execute.

Remove Distractions – Distractions in your work day are the single most destructive thing to our effectiveness and why getting things done often is a challenge. Many of us have an open door policy and it is likely appropriate. If you are still reading this book, (I am ever grateful that you are), you are likely one of those people that many in your workplace and family depend on. That being said, they also depend on you getting things done, and constant distractions destroy your flow of execution. The best way to handle this is to use break away sessions. Break away sessions allow you to schedule time to close your door (if you have one) and focus on executing off of your task list. Try to make it the same time every day so people know not to come by your desk or office at that time. If you wish, you can hang a small dry erase board or sign, saying, 'Leave your name and I'll look you up when I get done.' This way no one is offended and you get to finish your tasks. If you are unsure of where the distractions are coming from, use our Distraction Collector Tool found in the appendix. Other types of distractions like your smart phone, the internet and other gadgets we might have that steal our focus are productivity killers. I like to use the 20 second rule to take care of these. Make those things that distract you 20 seconds harder to get to. For instance, place your smart phone across the room, put it on silent and charge it up (whether it needs it or not) and make it more difficult to get to. Then focus on the task. The reverse works just as well by the way. Make the things that you need to get done easier to get to, and you will experience success. Every night I lay out my clothes for my workout and this makes me much more likely to go to the gym.

Beast Mode — Occasionally you need to let the inner beast of productivity out of its cage. You will notice this at work on those days before your vacation when you are trying to do five day's work in one day. The strange thing is, most of the time, it gets done! This tells us that a short burst of execution can work wonders in getting things done. I will point you back to one of my favorite books, *The Power of Full Engagement*. Schedule these beast mode sessions and go hard for a short period of time, much like an elite athlete might train and how *The Power of Full Engagement* suggests we should work. Be sure to allow yourself a break afterward though as rest after a beast mode session is necessary for mental recovery. I typically do this right before I leave for lunch. This gives me ample time to refuel my body and my mind. If you are a project manager or a software programmer, you may have heard this called a sprint session or a scrum. The concepts are the same. How do you get into beast mode? Do the following:

- Gather everything you need — pens, documents, ideas, notes, dry erase board, etc.

- Set a timer — You are going to be going hard here so make sure this is for no more than an hour or two. I have found the folks who have the physical conditioning to get through this are far better in a sprint session.

- Cue up some music — Music does wonders for me, and I also have my lucky bat that I use to practice my swing as I think through an idea!

- Turn off the phone! — There is no need to explain this.

- Prepare the body — Get warmed up as if you were about to jog 5 miles. Take some breaths, stretch the body, swing the lucky bat a few times and get ready to unleash the beast.

- Sketch out a plan — nothing elaborate here, just the items you need to complete.

- Express what ideality looks like — Get in the right mindset by expressing out loud 3 specific ways you can get the absolute best results for what you are about to do.

- Unleash the beast!

Try to do beast mode at least 1 time per week, but make sure it is for a worthy issue because beast mode does take energy from the body. Not because the individual effort is so taxing, you will find you are invigorated and hyped the rest of the day, and will push your body after a session like this even more when it is over. You will likely need to rehydrate and it is possible you may want to start a late night meditation session or some other method of relaxation when you get home, because you will still be in a heightened state long after the sprint session has ended. Typically a beast mode session feeds productivity the rest of the day and week. I would compare this to high-intensity cardio training. When you participate in high- intensity cardio training the benefits of burning fat last much longer after the session is over and your body remains in the this heightened state of fat burn. Beast mode is similar in that sometimes I find my thought clarity and overall ability to use discernment increased after a beast mode session.

Continual Improvement — Look at your daily/weekly worksheets, if you are carrying tasks over for more than 3 days, chances are these are not important tasks or you need to buckle down here and seek improvement. We may need to clear to neutral or back up a step and change what the task request is as you may not have the information needed to complete it. Be sure to value the small wins when you can and make sure that you find a reward system that works for you.

CHAPTER **14**

The Corporate Connection

"Before you are a leader, success is all about growing yourself.
When you become a leader, success is all about growing others."
—Jack Welch

OBVIOUSLY YOU CAN see the connection between Life Planning and how it leads to improved execution at your job or within your career. I wanted to at least spend some time discussing how this system can be overlaid in the corporate world, but rest assured we have already begun the initial outline for our book, *Enhanced Corporate Performance*, and if you are an entrepreneur or a leader in your company, it will be a must read. We have an entire consulting practice that utilizes this process and we have offered it for some time. Many people along the way have asked me why I didn't start with the corporate book first and my answer is simple. Companies are made up of people. If people are not fulfilled and truly in touch with where the Holy Spirit wants them to be, then how well could the company really be doing? Take the time to find people who are in alignment with what the universe wants for them and they will become leaders within your organization, regardless of their job responsibility. Otherwise you have a company full of 'lost' people and their decision making skills are not likely to be on point either. Dave Ramsey, talk show host and author of *Financial Peace,* along with countless other

accomplishments, lives out this process even in their hiring practices. Their company resides in Nashville, and since I spend quite
a bit of time there I have run into numerous people who work for
Mr. Ramsey or went through the interview process with him. They
are relentless in making sure that you not only have the skillset that
it takes to accomplish the job, but that you and your family are in
the right place spiritually to accomplish the job and that the job will
help to enhance your family. Great job here, Dave!

I do have one more commercial if you would allow, Enhanced
Performance is also working on a software program that will enable
companies to utilize our system in a manner that sets clear criteria
for all members of the team to be successful. It will facilitate input
from the entire company, and give unparalleled power to managers
and directors. If you would like to be kept abreast of our progress
here, please email me at dmonistere@enhancedlifeperformance.
com.

In corporations today, many have grown quickly because of a
great product or service. What began as a mission to provide the
best product or service to serve a specific need quickly becomes a
race to satisfy the stakeholders instead of focusing on what made
them successful. The one thing companies should always ask when
providing a product or service. You guessed it… Why? Why are we
even providing this service to begin with? What is our mission, what
is our vision, and what is our unique value proposition? More importantly, is what we are doing in line with what the universe wants for
this company? This all sounds really familiar I know, and it doesn't
follow the path of the Enhanced Life Performance Plan all the way
through, but it is very similar. Since I will have an entire book on
this subject, and the software that we are creating pretty much walks
you through the entire thing, I will give you the highlights.

You must have the following to be successful in business today:

Core Purpose — What is your mission, your vision, and the values of the organization that are non-negotiable?

Key Initiatives — What are the key initiatives that the company as a whole is working towards?

Milestones — What milestones are you trying to reach within this year, ½ year and quarter?

Resources – What do you have at your fingertips to use to hit these milestones? This include personnel and mechanical, software and other tools.

Play Book - What does the playbook say about the plan to hit those milestones and key initiatives?

Practice — What are you doing to prepare to win once you execute? In the corporate world, this typically deals with your company training plans.

Game Plan — What is the game plan for the next quarter?

Plays — What specific plays are you running in that game plan, and who are your field generals that are taking you into battle?

The Score — Are you winning?

Who is benefiting? — Who benefits when your company is doing well? Charity and corporate responsibility has become popular as of late, but corporations that do not having a symbiotic relationship with the universe that it exists in will point to its ultimate demise. Enhance first the communities you serve, and then look further out into the world and allow your company's success to benefit others through charity.

Everyone knows that I am an athlete, and yes, this is typically how coach's get ready for a big game. I am here to tell you, most coaches and their players are more prepared to win than most CEO's and their staff ever are. Follow this plan and every arm chair quarterback at your company will engage like never before.

If you are wondering how we do our corporate executive coaching, this is a good guide to how it looks, and of course the book that we have recently started will go into much greater detail. If you should choose to hire one of our executive coaches, what transpires in those bi-monthly visits is nothing short of miraculous. Many successful companies, despite their lack of direction, have experienced a new found focus that the company either never had, or lost as they grew. More importantly, many members of the executive team found themselves more fulfilled than they had ever been at their company before, or any one previous to that.

In short, these concepts work because it is all about alignment with what your company is supposed to be, and what they are supposed to do, all while finding a way—even a small way—to give back to the community they have prospered in; regardless of the size or area that the community they support has become. If enough companies do this, the result becomes successful companies producing a sense of community, allowing everyone to progress both within and outside of the organization.

CHAPTER **15**

Conclusion

"The end is never the end. It's always the beginning of something."
— Kate Lord Brown

WE HAVE COME a long way and you have consumed a large amount of data. Putting this to good use is difficult at times, and in the appendix I have added a special gift for you that we give at our coaching seminars. I have summarized all of the action steps in an easy to read step by step process. I have also included a glimpse into one of our life workbooks that we use during our Enhanced Life Program's Legacy Planning session to give you an idea of how to get started. Both of these items will help you begin on your own, creating an Enhanced Life that will put you in alignment with exactly what you were supposed to be doing all along. If you were already aligned, life will still get far easier because I have no doubt that you have likely picked up at least a few new ideas that you will turn into habit. That being said, for those who were out of alignment, you will feel as if a weight has been lifted and life has become far easier to lead.

There was a time in my life, where I thought I had finally created a life that I just couldn't possibly lead or execute on. Everything was hard! Everything was difficult to complete or maintain, and more importantly, I couldn't think about legacy because I was too busy just trying to get through the day. Once I understood the power of the Enhanced Life Program's Legacy Plan and was prodded by a colleague to write it all down, things became so much better that it opened my eyes to many things in my world that I had been missing. I once thought I was too busy to get through the day and yet, once I achieved alignment with the Holy Spirit, my productivity went through the roof.

I hope you have enjoyed this book and that at some point in my life, I get the opportunity to serve you in some way. If you would like to give me your feedback or ask any questions, please send me an email at dmonistere@enhancedlifeperformance.com.

Appendix

I have included this appendix to hopefully summarize the process so that you will have a condensed version of what you should be doing immediately. Let me warn you, not reading the book and going straight to the appendix is a bad idea! Get the feel for the book and the logical progress that it follows, and you will be better prepared to come back to this appendix and start the process. Again, if you need one of our coaches to walk you through the process, feel free to contact me at dmonistere@enhancedlifeperformance.com.

Why?

Why? We asked this question when we were 4 years old almost as frequently as we asked for sweets. We were told no to the candy, and eventually no to the question 'Why!' To which we asked again, Why? Somewhere along the way our parents told us that asking 'why' was bad. The constant 'Why' questioning was irritating and it hasn't become any less so to us as adults, even though now we are the ones asking, but knowing the answer to this is truly the secret to how we progress through the difficult times. Knowing the reason behind it all makes those days when you feel it can't be any worse rewarding to persevere through and beyond.

Prep for Core Purpose and 6 areas of fulfillment

It is time for you to be the fly on the wall at your own funeral and listen in on what your family and friends are saying about you. You may remember these statements in Chapter 1. This is where you begin to find the common things that you feel are important to you.

1. In my lifetime I want to accomplish _____

_____.

2. In my lifetime I want _____,

_____, and _____ to know that I am

_____.

3. In my lifetime I want my immediate family to know me as

_____ and _____.

4. In my lifetime I want strangers to know me for

_____.

5. If I could give the world one thing back (service to the community, knowledge of some topic, teaching a Sunday school class) as a thank you for all of the great things I have been blessed with and had the discipline to nurture, it would be

_____.

To help you with 'The Why' we will go through numerous exercises to find that core purpose we know we are here for. Take five minutes and write down the following. Assume you are at your funeral, your immediate family, your wife, kids and parents are sitting down and the conversation is all about you! What do you want them to say about you?

The next exercise will tax your memory, but it is necessary to help zero in on the 'Why' and your core purpose. Try to look back on your life and remember when you were given a compliment or recognition that lifted you emotionally, or for that matter spiritually. What happened, and describe your feelings in detail.

Building the Virtual Dream Team — We should all strive to surround ourselves with a sphere of influence in our lives. These people that influence us will say a lot about who we are, and for that matter, who we will become. At Enhanced Life Performance we use something called the virtual sphere of influence to allow ourselves the best team ever created to help us through our lives. This creative process will teach you something about yourself and about how others might approach your hurdles, opportunities or road blocks.

Use the following 6 categories or 'areas of fulfillment' to start your virtual team.

Faith —

Family —

Career —

Financial —

Community—

Performance-

Charity—

Self-Evaluation– It is always good to take inventory of whom or what you feel you have become. Being truthful and honest with yourself is incredibly important in our next exercise. Ask yourself these three questions, and once you get back to your loved ones compare their answers about you that you listed for yourself.

    1. *What is the most valuable attribute or characteristic that I have with regard to my family, friends and community?*

    2. *What one thing or group of things that I do that has kept me from being a better version of myself?*

    3. *If there was one thing that I could change about myself, what would it be?*

Now that you have completed these tasks, you can begin your attempt at developing who you are and, more importantly, who you wish to become. Remember you must establish a connection with the Holy Spirit to guide you through the next statements, because this will help to establish your Legacy Plan!

Core Purpose –

Epitaph –

Family Statement –

Stranger Statement -

T-shirt slogan -

Mental Imagery -

When you begin this process of writing down the things that you wish to have in your life, you must verify that you own this process and own the things you are asking for. You must speak it aloud and prepare to accept it. You have to place yourself in a condition where you believe in your heart and mind that you 'WILL' accomplish these things instead of an emotional state of you 'trying' to accomplish them.

I will leave a legacy!
I will be fulfilled!
I will mentor and coach!
I will help people laugh and smile!
I will be a great father, husband and friend!
I will be a trusted advisor!
I will be respected in the community!
I will be in alignment with the Holy Spirit!
I will make my body a precision tool of execution!
I will be a warrior for the weak and less fortunate!
I will take and maintain extreme ownership of my life.

6 Areas of Fulfillment Template

Faith

In five years, I will have achieved a level of faith I have never before achieved in the past. The level of fulfillment and power that it gives me is unmistakable. The specific things about my faith that have improved and the milestones I have reached over the past years are proof of my progress. I humbly recognize that I am better for it. It all started when I _____

_____

_____ (remember this has yet to happen, but be descript as if it already has occurred) and the moments along the way where I stopped to look back and witness the improvement of my faith, and humbly thank the Holy Spirit for His guidance were __

_____

_____

_____. It proved to me that faith is a major component of fulfillment, and I know that my spirit, mind and body are acting in unison to provide the most fulfilled life that I can have, so that I can focus on giving back to this universe that has provided me so much. The three things about my faith that I am most thankful for and will continue to nurture are _____, _____ and _____. These three areas of my life will continue to feed me with an abundant source of energy and contentment that will satisfy my need to give back to the other 5 areas of fulfilment.

Family

In five years I will have a rich family life that transcends anything I imagined. The level of fulfillment and power that it gives me is unmistakable, and the specific things about my family that have improved, and the milestones I have reached over the past years are proof of my progress, and I humbly recognize that I am better for it. It all started when I _____

_____ _(remember this has yet to happen, but be descript as if it has already occurred)._ _The moments along the way where I stopped to look back and witness the rich deep connection that I have with my family and humbly thank the Holy Spirit for His guidance were_

_____. _It proved to me that my family is a major component of fulfillment and I know that my spirit, mind and body are acting in unison to provide the most fulfilled life that I can have, so that I may focus on giving back to this universe that has provided me so much. The three things I am most thankful for and will continue to nurture to improve the family bond and rich experience that we all currently share are_ _____, _____ _and_ _____, _and these three areas of my life will continue to feed me with an abundant source of energy and contentment that will satisfy my need to give back to the other 5 areas of fulfilment._

Career

I recognize that my faith and my family are major components of living a rich and fulfilled life. Progressing in both of these areas of fulfillment is necessary in order to impact my career and continue to sharpen the focus on the 'why' of my vocation. In 5 years I will have achieved a new and more advanced status, and a level that I have never before achieved in the past will soon be reached. The level of fulfillment and power that it gives me is unmistakable, and the specific things about my career that have improved and the milestones that I reached over the past years are proof of my progress. I humbly recognize that I am better for it. It all started when I _____

_____ _(remember this has yet to happen, but be descript as if it has already happened) and the moments along the way where I stopped to look back_ *and witness the positive outcomes within in my career, and humbly thank the Holy Spirit for His guidance were*

_____

_____. *It proved to me that faith and family are major components of fulfillment, and I know that my spirit, mind and body are acting in unison to provide the most fulfilled life that I can have, so that I may focus on giving back to universe that has provided me so much. The three skills that I am most thankful for and will continue to hone are* _____, _____ *and* _____ . *These three skills are necessary for continual improvement within my career, and are gifts to me from the Holy Spirit. I will continue to use the abundant source of energy that exists to find higher levels of execution so that the success that follows is unmistakable. This will ultimately enhance the feeling of fulfillment within my life and will feed my need to give back to the other 5 areas of fulfilment.*

Financial

I recognize that financial stability is a major component of living a rich and fulfilled life. I will have to delay gratification from time to time and follow a strict plan that allows me to have the necessities of life and in many cases those material things that allow me the opportunity to increase the efficiency of life. Money is merely a tool of fulfillment, not a measure of who or how successful I am. In five years I will have reached a level of financial well-being that allows me to focus on fulfillment and not be concerned with the pressures of financial needs to live. I will live below my means and amass a financial position that allows me to participate in community and charity only enjoyed by those who plan in that manner. My approach will be deliberate and with purpose. My financial position will provide a level of fulfillment and power that is unmistakable, and not to create a life of excess, but to share a life of abundance with those less fortunate who will in turn share with others as well. In five years I will have _____ *in my emergency account because it is my* *responsibility to my family. I will_____*

_____

_____ *(remember this has yet to happen, but be descript as if it has already happened) and the moments along the way where I stopped to look back and witness the positive outcomes within in my career and the decisions I made that has given me a life of abundance were_____*

_____ . *I know that the stresses of money are material, worldly stresses that will not enter into my life. I will live well beneath my means and practice charity when and wherever possible. I know that my spirit, mind and body are acting in unison to provide the most fulfilled life that I can have so that I may focus on giving back to those less fortunate that are interested in improving themselves, but just need an opportunity to do so. The three disciplines that I will continue to hone for continual improvement of my financial position in life are _____, _____ and _____. These three disciplines that are gifts to me from the Holy Spirit will continue to provide for me and my family in a manner that will allow me to achieve an exceptional life that is as much a joy as it is a responsibility. I will become a financial warrior for those who need the help by providing opportunity for those that wish to improve their position with their family and the Holy Spirit. This ultimately provides a feeling of fulfillment within my life and will feed my need to continue to seek out these important relationships in my community and give back to the other 5 areas of fulfilment.*

Community

I recognize that my community is a major component in living a rich and fulfilled life. Providing for my community and seeking out relationships within it is necessary for me to grow as a person and achieve a high level of fulfillment within my life. In 5 years I will have achieved a new and more advanced status in my community, a status that has never before been achieved by me in the past. The level of fulfillment and power that it gives me is unmistakable. It all started when I _____

_____

_____ (remember this has yet to happen, but be descript as if it has already happened) and the moments along the way where I stopped to look back and witness the positive outcomes that were created through this were _____

___

_____

_____ . It proved to me that relationships within my community are major components of fulfillment and I know that my spirit, mind and body are acting in unison to provide the most fulfilled life that I can have so that I may focus on giving back to the universe that has provided me so much. The three things that I can point to where I have made a positive impact over the past five years are _____, _____ and _____. These three outcomes that are gifts to me from the Holy Spirit will continue to impact the community in a manner that will outlive me and my time on earth. This ultimately provides a feeling of fulfillment within in my life and will feed my need to continue to seek out these important relationships in my community and give back to the other 5 areas of fulfilment.

Charity

In five years I will have achieved a level of fulfillment in my family that will allow me to focus on charity for others. The level of fulfillment and power that it gives me is unmistakable, and the specific things about my acts of charity that have improved and the milestones I have reached over the past few years are proof of my progress, and I humbly recognize that I am better for it. It all started when I _____

_____

_ (remember this has yet to happen, but be descript as if it has already *happened) and the moments along the way where I stopped to look back and witness the charitable things that I have accomplished were so incredibly rewarding that it almost seemed as if I were doing them for my own immediate family. I humbly thank the Holy Spirit for His guidance as he showed me that charity can provide me fulfillment. The most rewarding charitable project I worked on this year was__ _____. It proved to me that charity is a major component of fulfillment, and I know that my spirit, mind and body are acting in unison to provide the most fulfilled life that I can have, so that I may focus on giving back to the universe that has provided me so much.*

Guide to Meditation

To try and simplify this process I will give you the 4 steps that have helped me. I find meditation to be very personal so I was hesitant to list anything, and instead, ask you to do your own research on this, but this is something you would have likely found anyway.

Step 1 — Take 3 deep breaths using your diaphragm to bring air in and push air out. Try not to take shallow breaths, these are full slow breaths (and shouldn't make a bunch of noise.)

Step 2 — Focus all of your attention on the present and be mindful of the peacefulness of the present moment. Begin the process of thanking the Holy Spirit for all that you have been given.

Step 3 — Starting with your feet, try and relax every muscle and tendon, making sure you feel comfortable. I try to go from the bottom up and focus on each body part.

- Feet
- Ankles
- Calves
- Knees
- Quads

- Hips
- Lower back and lower abdomen
- Upper back and chest
- Shoulders
- Arms
- Neck
- Head

As you travel up the body, envision an energy field or aura that surrounds those parts and accept that the aura is peaceful with the intent to help you find your center and be in communion with the Holy Spirit.

Step 4 — Once you have relaxed these parts of your body, be thankful for the gift of each of these body parts. Release anything that is nagging you from a pain perspective to that aura or energy field that surrounds you. At this point you should be in a very peaceful state, try and remain in that moment and invite the Holy Spirit to be present and sit with you. If you are a nonbeliever you can ask that the universe open its arms and be in communion with you. As you exit meditation, take three breaths again, but as you release them imagine that the negativity you hold is carried away with every breath that leaves your body. Remember to be patient with this process and practice, practice, practice!

Guide to Humility

1. Take responsibility for your misgivings that cause strife and apologize with an admonishment to do better.
2. Accept daily irritations with good humor.
3. Be courteous and delicate even when provoked.

Guide to Spiritual Connection

1. **Define what the Spirit is to you** — I have a very strong faith and my thoughts of the Spirt is that of the Holy Spirt, part of the Trinity, but that doesn't mean that the Spirit can't manifest itself within me as 'my' soul! This is important, because you must know what you believe the Spirit is to you. To me, the Spirit is both external and internal. To clarify once again, I see the Holy Spirit as something outside of me that I can access through prayer, meditation and seeking community with daily. The soul is the manifestation of my supernatural spiritual core. In fact, for me I believe it has physical properties, only ones we can't detect on an MRI or XRAY; my spirit is the 'output' of my soul that has been nourished through my efforts with the Holy Spirit. Simply stated, the soul is what you and God have made as the driver of your mind and body!

2. **Give the Spirit a physical manifestation in your mind** — As I mentioned before, the more we give physical properties to the things that are not visible, the better defined and more easily accessible they become to us. The Holy Spirit has a very specific physical manifestation for me, I am positive it was placed there over the years of my Catholic, Christian upbringing. God, within my mind, is a regal entity in a flowing robe sitting on a throne with Jesus at his right hand. Wondering where that image came from? If you are not sure look up, "The Apostles Creed." Surrounding both God and Jesus is a shroud of light that engulfs the entire scene in my mind, and at the top is a white dove whose feathers surround God and Jesus in a protective blanket that is beautifully soft and seems to have life like a flowing stream. When I call on the Holy Spirit during prayer, the image never changes, but when I seek communion with the Holy Spirit, the image changes to the childlike Jesus that I mentioned earlier, and sits next to me to

help mold and shape my soul. It is likely that I find this image less intimidating and it seems easier for me to ask for the help and knowledge of an all-knowing child.

3. **Engage the Spirit daily** — Lastly, do this on a daily basis if you can. I am a martial arts instructor, and for 6 years of my life, I prepared fighters to enter various MMA tournaments. We used to say that the only way to learn how to fight is to fight, the same holds true here. To get good at this you have to do it... a lot! You will suck at this for a long time, but the clearer those images become in your mind's eye, the easier it will become. Meditation is a learned process and you do get better the more that you do it. You will find creative ways to fit this into your day and if you put your mind to it and use the steps given earlier in this chapter, engaging the Holy Spirit daily becomes a very rewarding experience.

The Three Brain Phases and How to be Mindful

In order to control the mind, we need to delve deeper into how we react to things within and around us. There are three phases that we go through when the mind begins to interact with its surroundings.

Awareness – The mind is aware because it utilizes its 5 senses to place it in this state of awareness. Factors like sensations, smells, tastes and something as abstract as perceptions all work with the mind to accomplish this.

Consciousness – Awareness must exist before we can be conscious of it. Consciousness takes the awareness to a different level. It begins to play out how your spirit, mind, and body might choose to interact with what you have become aware of. For instance, you might say that I am now aware that my wife is home from work, so I am going to greet her, kiss her and ask her how her day went. This is the deliberate thought of what you might do about the awareness. The final phase is integration.

Integration – Integration is the executing of the plans made by the conscious mind to interact or integrate with the thing that you were made aware of.

So our focus as we work to improve the connection with the mind should be as follows:

1. Accept what mindfulness is and work to understand how we can impact every function of the brain. After all, it is your brain!

2. Accept that the Holy Spirit or the Universe has dominion over your soul and spirit, and that your spirit should be allowed dominion over the mind

3. Accept that relationships are the key to nourish and enhance your mindfulness experience, placing you squarely in the middle of the positive or negative energy of the Universe.

So how do we utilize this to improve mindfulness?

I have developed these 7 steps over the years of trying to hone the state of extraordinary mindfulness, and this undoubtedly will help get you to a new state of mind and state of being.

1. Practice Focus

2. Develop a plan of Integration for repetitive situations

   - Introductions

   - Meeting new people

   - Delivering praise

   - Delivering bad news

3. Meditation with a focus on mindfulness and being in the moment only (we will not engage the Holy Spirit here, He is already there)

4. Slow down!

5. Do something creative and interesting that tests your skills, this helps us to be 'present' in the moment.

6. Seek out positive relationships and be in the moment when engaging those relationships.

7. And finally,

8. Using Neuroplasticity to our advantage

The Body

Remember I promised you a practical approach to tapping into a new way of living your life. These 3 steps are as practical as it gets and although many of the things that we have talked about in previous chapters require the ability to do things that you have likely never done before, these 3 steps are more about having the desire and discipline to do it.

- Nourish The Body
  - » Eat Raw Organic Foods
  - » Cook with natural sources of heat and as little of it as possible
  - » Learn the messages your body is sending and eat only when hungry
  - » Balance your macronutrients
- Rest The Body
  - » 8 hours of sleep – this is different for everyone, but good rule of thumb
  - » Listen to the body for signs of diminished recovery
- Test The Body
  - » Push past failure
  - » Push your mental capacities as well
  - » Rest

Fats Breakdown

Saturated Fats or trans fatty acids	Polyunsaturated Fats	Monounsaturated Fats
Butter	Corn oil	Canola oil
Lard	Fish oils	Almond oil
Meat, lunchmeat	Soybean oil	Walnut oil
Poultry, poultry skin	Safflower oil	Olive oil
Coconut products	Sesame oil	Peanut oil
Palm oil, palm kernel oil and products	Cottonseed oil	Avocado
Dairy foods (other than skim)	Sunflower oil	Olives
Partially hydrogenated oils	Nuts and seeds	Peanut butter

The Three-Year Plan

I find that my strength in faith is tested regularly and my ability to remain positive and focused on the word to be a challenge. I know to be congruent with the Holy Spirit, I must continue to seek out humility and keep my own ego in check. Reading the word is essential to maintain that level of humility and a humble servant mentality that is necessary to leave a legacy. Material things provide me nothing here on earth or in the next life. Lastly, while I don't wear my faith on my sleeve or preach to others, I need to feel more comfortable sharing my testimony and letting others know how powerful the Holy Spirit can be in their lives.

Keeping the level set statements in mind, I list these three key initiatives for my three-year plan.

- *Read the Word – There is no excuse not to read the one book that truly sets the tone for how we should lead our lives. God does not change and nor does the true nature of mankind. For this reason, the bible can set the truth in perspective even in times when things seem so out of sync with the rest of the universal powers that the Holy Spirit commands. I will be engaged in a bible study with men who share similar mindsets, and some who challenge me to go further in my faith!*

  » *How will I measure my success? I want to have a deep understanding of the word and I must be in the word to do so. I will achieve the following:*

    I will read from the bible daily and my three-year plan is to have joined a bible study that both informs and challenges me to have a deeper relationship with The Holy Spirit and His word. I will track daily my task of reading the bible, and at the end of each quarter measure whether I am achieving what I had hoped from the bible study.

- *Share my testimony – I have always been relatively private when it comes to my faith. I will purposefully seek out people who need to be exposed to the word and share my testimony with those who need to hear it.*

  » *How will I measure success? In order to share my testimony, I must be in a position to do so at the right place and right time. I will record each time I have made a connection with someone spiritually and strive to have accomplished this at least 3 times per quarter.*

- *Increase my focus on Jesus' message of humility – Often times I lose sight of why I achieve at the level that I do. It is not because of me; it is because the Holy Spirit allows me to do so. Keeping this message of humility is difficult for me because I depend on what I think of as 'my will.' Or 'my discipline.' Neither of these attributes are mine to own, they are gifts from the Holy Spirit and I will continue to thank Him for these gifts.*

» *How will I measure success? In my daily reading I will always end with giving thanks to the Holy Spirit for the gifts He has given me, ask for forgiveness when I have allowed my ego to tell me that I am anything without God, and ask for guidance when showing others to be confident and never quit seeking the legacy that we wish to be. At each quarterly legacy review I will evaluate my prayer and meditation sessions and verify that thankfulness and humility is the strongest focus in each.*

This year I will accomplish many things, in the fulfillment area of 'Faith.' I will focus on three key initiatives which include reading the word, sharing my testimony and remaining humble in times where confidence and command are needed. I will achieve this because my plan is a focused approach to leaving a legacy after I am gone.

- The single most important thing that I wish to achieve this year in the key initiative of reading the word is first to utilize the book, *Power Thoughts Devotional*, by Joyce Meyer, to read daily and, at the end of each week, spend 15 minutes researching the power thoughts of the week.

  » *I will measure that I am effective in this endeavor by placing it as one of my 'quick hits' tasks (more on this later) so that I know I must accomplish it each day. In my quarterly 'Legacy Review' I will track how often I missed and make improvement if needed.*

- *The single most important thing that I wish to achieve this year in the key initiative of sharing my testimony is to take the opportunity when I feel the moment is right to share my testimony and trials that I have gone through to seek a deeper connection with the community that I serve. I realize that some attempts will not create that spiritual connection that I seek, but it is my goal to do so at least 3 times per quarter.*

» *I will measure my effectiveness to see if between each Legacy Plan Review that I have made a deep spiritual connection at least three times. I understand that in order to reach this goal I may have to attempt this more than ten or fifteen times in a quarter which must be tracked. If I have not reached three deep spiritual connections I will increase the number of times I will attempt it.*

- *The single most important thing that I wish to achieve this year in the key initiative of remaining humble and practicing humility is to not be defensive or seek out excuses or explanations when someone is asking me to change the way that I approach something, or when they are criticizing how I have behaved. All too often, great advice is given and I choose not to hear it because I am not approaching the conversation with humility. I will remain mindful that even though not all criticism is constructive, there is something within that person's word that I need to own.*

» *I will in my quarterly Legacy Plan Review track the number of times that I have committed to approach a situation differently. I will record this in my daily task sheet in the legacy portion of the sheet and study it during my Legacy Plan Review.*

The One-Year Plan with Resources

- *The single most important thing that I wish to achieve this year in the key initiative of reading the word is first to utilize the book,* **Power Thoughts Devotional,** *by Joyce Meyer, to read daily and at the end of each week spend 15 minutes researching the power thoughts of the week and spending more time in the word looking at how the various texts treat each of those thoughts.*

» *I will measure that I am effective in this endeavor by placing it as one of my 'quick hits' tasks so that I know I must accomplish it each day. In my quarterly 'Legacy Review' I will track how often I missed and make improvement if needed.*

» *Resources Needed: my bible (at home and at work), community bible study group, my wife, my children, community with the Holy Spirit, spiritual strength, discipline, time (well-planned schedule) my daily task list, and my mental faculties to comprehend what the word means to me.*

The Legacy Plan Review

The review is a simple three step process: Did you hit the goal? Did the goal meet its intended outcome? How can you improve it? Using the goal of my intent to improve on public prayer, this is a snippet taken directly from one of my quarterly reviews.

Did you hit your goal? Please explain: *After reviewing the past quarter, I found that public prayer was not an easy task for me to complete at first. Once I was accepting of the fact that our goal for public prayer is never to be perfect or to seek approval from the people that might be in the room, I found this to be much easier. This goal was created in an attempt to increase my own level of humility, but I fear that the confidence it has created within me is not truly humble and more about the acceptance of men. I don't need that acceptance and this is counter to a humble approach. I* am not ready to remove this item from this category or remove it all together, but I will be more mindful that my public prayer should be an attempt to stir emotion in others instead of an increase in confidence of public speaking for me.

Did this goal stir something in you emotionally? Please explain: This did stir something emotionally within me, but I will admit not necessarily a spiritual impact as others might think, it was more for my own public confidence.

What can be added or taken away to increase the effectiveness or improve? As mentioned above, I must remember what the goal was created for and remain humble in my approach to conquer a fear of public prayer. I need to make sure that my prayer is aimed at helping others, not making me feel comfortable with the way others might think of me. It is not a performance, it is an emotional prayer.

The Five-year plan — The five year plan is summary statement that gives you a general direction for the goal that you were more detailed about in the 3 and 1 year plan. The first goal in my 5 year plan would read like this:

Five-year plan - Faith

In five years, I will have achieved a level of faith I have never before achieved in the past. The level of fulfillment and power that it gives me is unmistakable. The specific things about my faith that have improved and the milestones I have reached over the past years are proof of my progress. I humbly recognize that I am better for it. It all started when I focused in on my Legacy Plan and made a focused effort to accept the Holy Spirit and engage Him in prayer and the moments along the way where I stopped to look back and witness the improvement of my faith, and humbly thank the Holy Spirit for His guidance were when I left encounters with friends and family and openly discussed how my faith was guiding me and the heightened awareness to God's presence in and around me was helping me to *become a better person. It proved to me that faith is a major component of fulfillment, and I know that my spirit, mind and body are acting in unison to provide the most fulfilled life that I can have, so that I can focus on giving back to this universe that has provided me so much. The three things about my faith that I am most thankful for and will continue to nurture are my new found openness, the strength and focus it has brought me and more importantly the grace that I am granted. These three areas of my life will continue to feed me with an abundant source of energy and contentment that will satisfy my need to give back to the other five areas of fulfilment.*

In order to find fulfillment of Faith, I will Focus on Jesus' message of humility and surround myself with His word. All things can be achieved through the Father, the Son and the Holy Spirit and the Word will be my guide.

Your weekly schedule should look as follows:

Sunday Night — Take 15 minutes to organize the upcoming week. Set your weekly goals and set your tasks for Monday. If your daily tasks template is well laid out, this should not take very long to accomplish. It isn't necessary to have every detail of every day, Monday through Friday. Many of the supportive tasks will take some time to expose themselves to you over the first couple of days during that week.

Monday- Friday — At the end of each day you must prepare your tasks for the following day and evaluate your weekly progress towards the 6 areas of fulfillment. Again, be mindful of trends and do everything that you can to place yourself in the best position to be successful. I keep a pretty comprehensive food log and I have made some incredible discoveries about how my body reacts to certain foods and my overall performance throughout the week. I consider myself a bit of a biohacker so for me tweaking the body to perform at an optimal level is a bit of a hobby and I enjoy it. All I am asking here is for you to pay attention to trends that you see as the days unfold.

Friday Afternoon — The last hour of each Friday is YOUR TIME! Make sure that you take the time to evaluate your week. See what you accomplished and record any small wins or Legacy Impressions. Be sure to transfer your Legacy Impressions to your Legacy Impressions tracking system so that you may review them during your quarterly review. Legacy Impressions help build momentum and further support the fact that you are on the right track.

Saturday – REST! Don't look at this at all on Saturday and allow your life to be a bit more spontaneous and off of the structured approach that you take during the week. This follows the same concepts that we discussed in previous chapters about a focused approach to our daily tasks and an aggressive attack of your day. In order to do this consistently, our bodies must have an opportunity to rest.

The brain uses more energy than any other organ in our body and this fact further supports the necessity of having a good nutrition and meal plan. This means that not only do we have to fuel the body and mind correctly, but we must give it ample rest. This is why you should pick a day on the weekend to just be off the grid. I choose Saturday, because I like to review my previous week and prepare for the upcoming week on Sunday evenings. This means my Saturdays are utilized for rest only.

I have included the template that I use for my weekly and daily tasks. Remember how we got here and you will start to tie in why the utilization of this program allows us to have an extraordinary life. Nothing is happening randomly! We are planning our lives in detail, executing our plan, evaluating the effectiveness of those daily and weekly tasks and then making improvements to help facilitate a better outcome. The Enhanced Life Program works for corporate planning as well and starts with the Mission, Vision and Values of the company, but the plan must be detailed and strategic. If you are interested in contacting one of our coaches to lead a corporate session, please feel free to reach out to us at customerservice@enhancedlifeperformance. com.

Before moving on, I wanted to point out that I keep track of my weekly and daily tasks on paper. Every week I have a summary placed in my planner of the one year plan. I review it weekly as I look back on the previous week and begin planning for the following. This way I know that my 6 areas of fulfillment and the Main, Secondary and Supportive tasks that must be done are in keeping with the 1 year plan.

Let's dissect the worksheet and then talk about how we tie it into the plan.

Weekly Goals and the 6 Areas of Fulfillment – The 6 areas of fulfillment: Faith, Family, Career Financial, Community and Charity are core components of how we leave a legacy.

The Quick Hits - These are things that we must do every day 90% of the time. These tasks likely don't take long or they are part of your daily routine.

Big Task for the Day – The big task for the day is usually work or family related. It will likely feed your Financial, Family and Career categories of fulfillment and that is exactly what we are after. Make sure you accomplish this one task each day. This is your main responsibility for the day!

Secondary Tasks for the Day – Utilizing the 1,3,5 rule, these secondary tasks are usually smaller projects that tend to involve and depend on other people in our sphere of community influence.

Supportive Tasks for the Day – These are smaller tasks that you should allow yourself softer deadlines and flexibility for.

Notes – You will find the notes section in the template is never big enough. I typically have an entire page set aside for notes.

Weekly Goals for the 6 areas of life fulfilment:

This week I will :

Faith- _____

Family- _____

Career- _____

Financial- _____

Community- _____

Charity- _____

Todays tasks consist of:

Quick hits:

[ ] Journal [ ] Exercise [ ] Meditate [ ] Write for 15 [ ] Birthdays [ ] Encourage Someone [ ] Website [ ] Bible

1-3-5 Rule :

Big Task for the day:

    [ ] _____

3 tasks that must be done:

    [ ] _____

    [ ] _____

    [ ] _____

5 supportive tasks:

    [ ] _____

    [ ] _____

    [ ] _____

    [ ] _____

    { } Plan tomorrow's day _____

Small Wins \ Legacy Impressions

Date   **Daily Notes**

Steps for Execution - A well laid out plan and no execution will create limited results. The best way this was described to me is that anything multiplied by zero is still zero. If you planned for 2 days or 2 years, if you multiplied by zero execution, you get zero results.

1. Start with something significant first

2. Capture your tasks effectively

3. Remove hurdles

4. Remove distractions

5. Go Beast Mode

6. Continual Improvement

Do Something Significant First

USE THE ROLLER COASTER EFFECT TO POWER THROUGH YOUR DAY

What is the 'roller coaster effect'?

- Think of how a roller coaster works:
  - The first hill is a doozy - It takes a lot of time, energy, and effort to get over it - least fun part of the ride
  - After the first hill, momentum kicks in - Once you've overcome the first hill, the rest of the hills are easier to go over due to the *momentum* generated from getting past the first hill

Successful, productive days work the same way

- The order in which you complete tasks each day has the same effect
  - The first task is a doozy - When you do something significant first each day, it's going to be hard, take a lot of energy, and probably not going to be much fun
  - After the first task, momentum kicks in - Completing a significant task first *builds momentum* for completing the rest of your tasks more easily

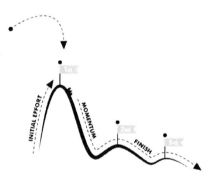

The effect of going the opposite direction

- On a roller coaster - The might easily get over the first few hills, but the last big hill would be virtually insurmountable due to a lack of momentum
- During your day - You might easily complete several small tasks, but by the end of the day, you'll lack the momentum to complete the big task that still needs done

Significant tasks to do first/small tasks to avoid

- Significant - Putting together a presentation, writing and publishing a blog post, or recording and editing a video or two
- Small - Reading the news, checking Facebook/Twitter, watering the plants

CHALLENGE/NEXT ACTIONS

- For the next 3 days in a row, work on something significant first - something that may take a lot of time/energy, or something you just don't enjoy doing
- Pay attention to how using this strategy affects your overall productivity

TODAY: WRITE IT DOWN...

TOMORROW: DO IT FIRST!

Capture Your Tasks Effectively

3 SIMPLE WAYS TO TURN YOUR TO-DO LIST INTO A <u>DONE</u> LIST

'Video' <--- what does it mean?!?

- Pick up a video?
- What is a video?
- Where can you watch a video?
- Who knows!

Guess what - your brain doesn't know either

- Your brain looks at this single word, wondering what to do with it

If this is how you capture tasks, stop it

- The number of unanswered questions about a task placed on your to-do list like this will affect your ability and desire to complete it:
  - Presentation?!?
  - Trip?!?
  - Proposal?!?

Here are 3 ways to turn to-do's into done's

- **Verbs** - These signal to your mind and body that it's time to get into 'action mode'
- **Details** - These provide clarity and remove resistance to taking action
- **Deadlines** - These increase your level of motivation to take action

Capture tasks the <u>right</u> way

- **Example:** *30 mins: Write a blog post about how to turn a to-do list into a done list:*
  - *Write* - Is a verb that describes the action required to complete the task
  - *Write a blog post about...* - Provides details about the goal of the task
  - *30 mins* - Gives the task a mini deadline to fuel taking action on it

CHALLENGE/NEXT ACTIONS

Update your to-do list, or begin a new list following these guidelines for each action item on the list:

- Begin it with an action word (Words) - *Create, make review, write, record, organize, etc.*
- Be specific about what needs done (Words) - So specific and detailed that you could hand the task off to someone else and they would know exactly what to do
- Include an estimated amount of time it will take to complete - A close estimation is good enough

---

VIDEO

Pick up video?

What is a video?

Where can you watch a video?

VERB

30 mins: **Write** a blog post about how to turn a to-do list into a done list

DETAILS

30 mins: Write **a blog post about how to turn a to-do list into a done list**

DEADLINE

30 mins: Write a blog post about how to turn a to-do list into a done list

How It Works: Distractions
REALIZE THAT THERE ARE NO SMALL DISTRACTIONS

There are no 'small' distractions

- There's often a misconception that some distractions aren't a big deal because *they take less than a minute* to handle:
  - Checking notifications
  - Answering 'quick' questions from co-workers
  - Responding to an email
- **The truth:** All distractions – *big* and *small* – have a huge impact on your overall productivity

It has less to do with using time, and more with destroying flow

- The impact that a distraction has on your ability to get things done has less to do with the length of time the distraction and more to do with the way it disrupts the flow of what you're already doing
- Each time you stop what you're currently doing in order to handle even a *small* distraction, there are 3 factors that come into play:
  - **The time it takes to slow down** – The time it takes to switch from what you're currently doing to handling the distraction
  - **The length of the stop** – The length of the distraction
  - **The time it takes to regain your momentum** – The time it takes to regain the 'speed' you were working on the task prior to the distraction.
    - This is often the most devastating factor of all
- Depending on how many distractions you allow to happen, this process can be repeated many times throughout your day, slowing your forward progress down considerably
- This is similar to driving your car in-town and stopping constantly for a few seconds at every *Stop* sign

It's better to keep your foot on the 'gas'

- This is opposed to simply being able to keep your foot on the gas – stopping every hour to handle a batch of 'distractions' at once, and getting back on the road again

WHY THIS MATTERS/HOW TO USE IT

- **Refuse to give into distractions** – including 'small ones' – unless absolutely necessary (if it can be taken care of later, as many things can, then do that) – set aside time each day to deal with these kinds of tasks (a **Break Away Session**).
- Don't destroy other peoples' momentum by creating distractions that can be dealt with at a later, more appropriate time!

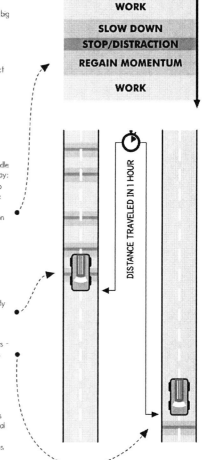

Tool: Distraction Tracker

DISCOVER AND ELIMINATE YOUR BIGGEST DISTRACTIONS

How to use this tool:

- Spend the next week being aware and tracking your distractions
- When you are distracted, take a second to note that distraction in the appropriate box below with a hash mark (I).
- At the end of the week, total the hash marks to identify your biggest distraction and one specific way to minimize/eliminate it
- NOTE: You'll notice that simply being aware that you're tracking your distractions will likely cause you to minimize them anyway.

✉ **Interacted with email**

	TOTAL

☎ **Interacted with the phone**

	TOTAL

☖ **Was interrupted by someone**

	TOTAL

f Checked or responded to social media

	TOTAL

🔍 **Surfed the Web**

	TOTAL

✨ **Cleaned or interacted with my environment**

	TOTAL

✳ **Misc.**

	TOTAL

My <u>worst</u> distraction is:

The <u>one specific action</u> I will take to minimize/eliminate this distraction is:

Use Beast Mode for Massive Results

UNLEASH YOUR INNER-BEAST TO GET LOTS OF THINGS DONE

Good is usually good enough

- If you manage your time and your life properly, then good, consistent results are going to generally make you happy

Sometimes, your inner-beast needs let out of its cage

- Occasionally you need to <u>unleash the productivity beast within you</u> to create massive results:
  - Vacation is coming up, and you need to get more done than you usually do
  - A deadline has been moved up on a project
  - You simply want to challenge yourself to see what you can do (one of my favorites)

Flip your switch to BEAST mode

- **Gather everything you need** - Pens, documents, ideas, notes, whatever
- **Set a timer** - For the duration of time you want to spend in BEAST mode
- **Cue up some energetic music** - Something that will get you pumped up and excited, but not distracted
- **Turn off everything** - Turn off your TV, phone, notifications - anything that has the potential to disrupt your flow and momentum
- **Prepare your body** - Get up and move/stretch a bit, and take several deep breaths
- **Sketch out a simple plan** - Create an outline of the steps you're going to take to complete what you need to do
- **Express what you know** - Get in the right mindset by expressing, out loud, 3 specific ways you can get the absolute best results for what you're about to do
- **Take action like a beast** - (Self-explanatory)

CHALLENGE/NEXT ACTIONS

- Experience **BEAST mode** at least 1 time this week, even if it's only for an hour - <u>discover the potential you have within you to get massive results!</u>

About The Author

Don Monistere can claim quite a diverse background. He has spent quite a bit of time honing his skills as a coach, mentor, martial arts instructor, fitness instructor, nutritionist and competitive bodybuilder, all while amassing 30 years of experience in various Information Technology business endeavors.

Monistere said recently "I gravitated to Information Technology because it is very similar to how I have approached sports, martial arts, coaching and many of the other endeavors in my life that don't seem related. The commonality between them all is the inputs and the outputs. Output can only be consistent if the input is consistent and the knowledge of why there should be an output in the first place must be fully understood!"

Monistere has taken this approach over many years of trial and error. "Not sure why I wasn't a Scientist." He said "I love to execute a given set of instructions based on certain goal oriented criteria, measure its success and then make improvements along the way." This is evident in his book *Enhanced Life Performance ... achieving the greatest version of self*. With continual improvement always in mind, Monistere walks us through the steps of how to become completely in line with what we were meant to do and how to leave a true Legacy behind while recording "Legacy Impressions" along the way, a concept he came up with to help monitor and measure his effectiveness at the creation of Legacy.

Currently; as the Chief Operations Officer at TekLinks, a regional

IT firm, Monistere has been given the responsibility of management and executive oversight of all areas of the Service Management System utilized to deliver services to the many customers within their foot print.

Monistere took on this role after founding and serving as the CEO of Vista Information Systems. Later selling his company to TekLinks which has become one of the dominate players in Managed and Cloud as well as other Information Technology related services.

He achieved his Bachelors of Science in Business Management from Southeastern Louisiana University and later Masters of Business Administration from Aspen University in Aspen Colorado where he became a distinguished member of the Delta Epsilon Tau Honor Society.

Monistere has owned three companies over the past 25 years, 2 technology based companies and one martial arts training center with 2 locations and currently works with his sons Cooper and Cameron Monistere as a consultant and coach for Enhanced Sports Performance while still managing to do coaching and consulting for Enhanced Life Performance as well.

He holds a 3rd dan-degree black belt in Kyokubougei Karate, which is a rare form of combat martial arts and works closely with student athletes in the Vestavia and Hoover community to provide structure and discipline that martial arts and other sports have taught him.

He attests his rigid process approach to his life and business as a direct result of his work in sports and of course with the guidance that he seeks from The Holy Spirit

CPSIA information can be obtained
at www.ICGtesting.com
Printed in the USA
FSOW01n1503280917
39250FS